THE
MONA LISA

THE ART OF WOMEN, AGE, AND POWER

STRATAGEM

THE
MONA LISA

THE ART OF WOMEN, AGE, AND POWER

STRATAGEM

HARRIET RUBIN

WARNER BOOKS

NEW YORK   BOSTON

Warner Books

Hachette Book Group USA

237 Park Avenue

New York, NY 10169

Visit our Web site at www.HachetteBookGroupUSA.com.

Printed in the United States of America

First Edition: May 2007

10 9 8 7 6 5 4 3 2 1

Warner Books and the "W" logo are trademarks of Time Warner Inc. or an affiliated company. Used under license by Hachette Book Group USA, which is not affiliated with Time Warner Inc.

Library of Congress Cataloging-in-Publication Data

Rubin, Harriet

   The Mona Lisa stratagem : the art of women, age, and power /
Harriet Rubin.—1st ed.

    p. cm.

 Includes bibliographical references

 ISBN-13: 978-0-446-57765-6

 ISBN-10: 0-446-57765-0

 1. Women—Psychology. 2. Women—Conduct of life. 3. Aging—
Psychological aspects. 4. Youthfulness. 5. Self-realization in women. I. Title.

 HQ1206.R74 2007

 155.3'33—dc22

                         2006035248

For Mona Rinzler

And for Betty Sue Flowers

Every age bears its fruits;

it's all in knowing how to

harvest them.

CONTENTS

Jackie's Immortal Godmothers—
Or, what a young woman sought in unwrapping
the gifts of maturity

The Stratagem:
Ageless and Timeless in Ten Tactics

Only the woman who has faced enormous
loss may proclaim herself first among the
immortals, because she is invulnerable to the
wounds inflicted by mere humans.

CONTENTS

Tactic Two / 47

In any situation in which you wish to be treated royally, be yourself, and others will play "the queen."

Tactic Three / 61

Become a great man who is all woman, because the sexes do not age. They mature into femininity.

Tactic Four / 72

The face of feminine command directs attention away from oneself and increasingly to others and to the world at large. Therein is found true sleeping beauty.

Tactic Five / 109

A liberal in thought, an autocrat in action, prudish in words, unbridled in deeds: this is the recipe for the leader who would submit like a girl and dominate like a woman.

CONTENTS

Tactic Six / 126

The body is subject to the forces of gravity. But the soul is ruled by levity. Master the depths of your mysterious smile, because a woman's laughter is more powerful than her tears.

Tactic Seven / 146

Hate and wait, because one doesn't grow strong on a diet of wimpy burgers. Do not fear critics or appease them. Rather, bring forth tigers out of their cocoons.

Tactic Eight / 165

Permit people moments of privileged madness. Permit them to feel their anger and sorrow—and to forget for a time so-called sweet reason. The voice of female gravitas doesn't want us to reason, but to see anew.

CONTENTS

Tactic Nine / 182

*Feed the flame of your charisma, because all who
stand before you wish to enter your circle.*

Tactic Ten / 212

*The art of the comeback requires
that you reject any attempt to be young and instead
make the old new.*

The Stratagem / 227

*Women are more themselves in age
than at any other time. They locate realms
of permanence in the world. They create love
that constantly renews itself. They engage
in actions that are impervious to forces of decay
and disintegration. By such means, Lioness
and Lamb become one, and the feminine
heart of leadership prevails.*

Where May We Find Great Leaders Today?

The answer is, in maturity. Founding fathers, old masters, and statesmen-presidents are vastly different from young go-getters—as different as lightning is from a lightning bug, to quote Mark Twain. Bach took his greatest leap of faith in maturity, creating music for an instrument, the clavier, not yet invented; and the founders wrote a Constitution that would mature over generations. "Mature" is a set of qualities—an adjective—but it is also a verb: to bring something to ripeness. Whenever Time moves unbearably fast, maturity becomes the corrective against disasters. Who are the experts on maturity but women?

You hold in your hands a *Prince* for grown-ups, an *Art of War* on how to face the last big enemy, Time, and Mortality, its evil twin. Women have perfected maturity: they reach that state sooner and enjoy it longer. This, then, is the first study of leadership for men and women in which the performance benchmarks are those of mature women. John McCain could, for example, take a lesson from Condoleezza Rice, who gets hyperarticulate and bristly when she is mad, but not bitchy—a style perfected by Elizabeth I, whose five-decade rule made England the center of the civilized world. Or Oprah, whose anger and ambitions often have a dignity like that of Golda Meir, the mature master-builder of national pride. Men, listen up: throughout history, great careers evolve into feminine endings.

The world itself may be evolving into a feminine ending: an ancient Sanskrit prophecy holds that at zero hour women will take power to avert the Earth's demise. In troubled, macho countries, women are being elected to the highest political offices because they represent change.

Which brings us to the great Leonardo—artist, engineer, alchemist, tutor to Renaissance kings: why, in his own maturity, did he hitch his star to the image of a woman, one of the most familiar and yet most mysterious ever seen—an icon that has kept him alive and venerated for more than five hundred years?

Jackie's Immortal Godmothers

Or, what a young woman sought in
unwrapping the gifts of maturity

A just-picked plum Jackie Kennedy—fresh and firm and all of thirty-one, new mistress of her husband's White House—developed an obsession for a chubby glamourpuss named Madame de Maintenon who was well past menopause when she secretly married a king (Louis XIV). It is said that to get at a French king, you had to wiggle through a wall of women. All the more extraordinary, then, that at the center one should find this grandmama, as if that word were adequate. At the age of seventy-five Madame complained to her priest that the king insisted on sex with her every day, sometimes several times. Madame had a commanding and seductive presence that was more irresistible than when she was young and lithe. She made herself the central figure wherever she appeared. The king who took as his emblem the midday sun felt humbled and overshadowed by her and suddenly aware of his own mediocrity. In a court of pose and pomposity, she remained modest, spiritual, and compelling.

It's obvious why a person might covet the insights of age and power late in life, but at thirty-one? Jackie wanted to get a head start on the practices of power at its greatest. Power is the most intoxicating thing in the world, and the most intoxicating power comes with maturity and the confidence of having seen and done everything. When one is stirred by a resurgence of creative energy rivaling that of earlier decades, the challenge lies in knowing how to channel that power to the best possible ends.

But a wizened old hen like Madame? Exactly like Madame! She was no slave to manbooze; she had love but was also free. At Madame's age, she could feel like a woman but luxuriate in the full force of her own mind, just like a man. She could be sour when cranky opinion moved her and an enlightened influence when truth was at stake. Her power went beyond having a king fall at her feet. A dozen or more women just like her became the original chattering classes: they opened salons in their homes, shaped the agendas for talk, lured into their midst the bright minds of the time, and used

THE MONA LISA STRATAGEM

these conversations to move ideas through the society. The ideas instigated by these "vintage" women and impregnated into men in high governmental and political positions formed a society distinguished by its insistence on truth and beauty. The Paris of the eighteenth-century *salonistes* became the center of the world and the inspiration for the French Revolution. Ben Franklin wooed the *salonistes* for their insight into politics and access to key figures. They had something going for them that had proved impossible even in their own youth, some magic formula that put them at the center like the noonday sun.

Power brokers who came after Madame de Maintenon established themselves at the center of the universe for one hundred years. Men today follow the principles of the Godfather. For a creative, less money-mad time, these women were Godmothers. They formed a loose confederation or matriarchy—circles within circles of power. They talked not only with men but avidly with each other. Their unity, formed of their adroit construction of social platforms, made them figures to be reckoned with. They became an army of women—a Taliban of women—out to reconstruct a society based on the most sublime peace, *amor mundi*: love of the world. They cherished people outside their families as they cherished members of their families. Because what one man or even one family could contain all they had to give? At an age when they might have disappeared into the shadows locked in isolation from a community of purpose, they took to the big stage of social, cultural, and political effectiveness. No wonder Madame captured the attention and admiration of the young Jackie Kennedy, who followed her example to invest herself as America's queen, a position she held for decades, until her death, no matter who succeeded her as First Lady.

Godmothers like Madame were the ultimate strategists. They could focus their attention upon improving the world because they knew who the *real* enemy was. Time! A young woman may be hooked, her energies drained, by a difficult husband, a paranoid boss, a jealous friend, or her own nasty ninjas of troubled self-confidence. But in age, such minor enemies lose their edge. They no longer confuse and distract. Rather, in age, one may act from a position of strength to confront and then to create a truce with Time. Time is the thief of youth, beauty, and assurance. Anything Time stole from Madame, however, she was happy to let go of: the tiny waist, the smooth neck, and the flock of children off to feather their own nests. She knew where to find compelling substitutes for whatever she lost. Jackie, who could have had herself tutored in power by any of the men in her husband's presidential court, chose her teachers carefully. Her Godmothers had a seventh sense men lack: *a sense of timing*. Let's put a finer point on it. They had a sense of how to live their lives not frozen in the glory of some distant past or with the promise of some faraway future. These women made the most of every moment. Age was a form of wealth for them, each passing year another deposit into accounts marked Cleverness, Spontaneity, Pleasure, Accomplishment, Ease!

The subject of women, age, and power opens a bold new frontier. The idea that age is increase in anything but devastation is new to us. Women now live longer than ever, and in many of them, much of the world's wealth is coming to reside, the consequence of widowhood and divorce. But power is a late-life acquisition: for female writers, for example, the act of self-creation comes later in life than for men. Men tend to move on a fairly predictable path to achievement; women transform themselves only after an awakening. What is the nature of women's late awakening? What powerful qualities show up late, like latecomers to a party who enliven the whole affair?

One's fifties are said to be one's most creative decade, one's sixties marked by freedom, and one's seventies by a state of nobility. But such talk seems like the myth of the no-calorie cheesecake. People say a bite won't cost anything, but you know it does. Age seems both the opposite of power and its deepest expression. How can it be both a huge gift and a high-ticket item?

The answer is that most people don't know how to age, but some people are better in age than they ever were. Age for those who get it right is a metaphysical diet: a chance to lose dead weight like the disease to please, the obsession with status, or the burden to be trendy or fashionable. In fact, everything Time steals means that something more important is restored.

Like Jackie, I set out to find those brilliant maturers, true alchemists of Time, and to understand the means by which they turned loss into tremendous gain. How did they continue walking into rooms and dazzling, no matter how many young women were present? Why did they grow more interesting, immune to disappearing into "the sands of time"? Why were they taken more seriously as leaders yet also considered more feminine than in their youth? How did they manage to work less and achieve more? The secret lay in a lost definition of femininity that is found in maturity.

I scoured hundreds of biographies to find this secret of how some women have aged brilliantly—have made the years between forty-five and ninety the best of their lives. One becomes the sum of one's parts in this second third of life. It is obvious, first of all, that maturity defines itself differently from youth, less in terms of success than in terms of happiness. People claim that life, liberty, and the pursuit of happiness is central to existence. But while there are plenty of defenders of life and liberty, how do we defend our right to be happy, which in maturity we crave? I saw common themes and actions in the lives of those who outsmart Time. They do not turn the clock back to mimic youth. Rather they live by the Stratagem. To do so, they practice the femininity lost to modern time. The Godmothers' Time-resistant feminine secrets as I found them unfold in these pages. They are immortal truths about how to approach being immortal, which is to mature to your sweetest, sharpest, and truest—and to rely on these ultra-feminine techniques for a very long time.

The women discussed herein are players: persons through whose hands the secrets of the whole world had to pass. I dismissed the notion that examples of great women are daunting to the rest of us. Why not have the best guides? Who looks at mediocre paintings for inspiration? Great pieces of art, though we may never fully understand them or how they were made, still invigorate and improve us.

I was interested especially in how in maturity a woman might fall in love with herself as a new experience so different from the plaguing uncertainties of youth. Central to this late-style power is how women negotiate the fear that no one is looking at them or appreciating them. Older, women are not invisible; rather, people look at them with a very different curiosity from that which greeted them in youth. Knowing the ways in which they are visible is a key to their power.

This book, then, is a primer of power. Primer as in basic work of strategy. Primer as in "first coat." Anything, any color, any design you cast over your life, love, and happiness will be brighter and more alluring because of how you keep the Stratagem's basic principles in mind.

· · ·

Maturity redefines the masculine virtues into a feminine key, which is what makes this a book of advice for both sexes. The wisdom of maturity is best summarized as gallantry. Gallantry is more than simply being good. Maturity shows respect for what is aesthetically appropriate or necessary. Gallantry is typically associated with men's actions toward women, which presumed a kind of delicateness on women's part. Female gallantry is protectiveness, resoluteness, love for ideals, and a maternal regard for the people in our charge, mixed with a light sense of irony, of taking oneself seriously *and* comically.

Everything about mature power is different from the so-called gold standard, which Machiavelli's *The Prince* and other classic works of effectiveness define as excitability, indelible action, and bringing events to a tragic boil or outcome, in which someone wins and others lose.

A new sense of Time and of timing changes one's worldview. For the young, the search is for the new-

new thing that must catch on quick. Mature ideas may also take on a disruptive quality but veer more toward the traditional: *a going against* the restless stream of innovation, not a desire for the unique but *a devotion to the irreducible thing*, that which endures, which is outside of Time and trends. This sounds difficult only because it is unusual. To position oneself beyond Time requires only a small shift in thinking. Instead of thinking of trends, observe how the irreducible is the Timeless element. It dazzles us with sheer beauty and rightness. The nurse Cicely Saunders went to medical school at age forty-five to become credentialed as a doctor because she wanted the respect necessary to establish as a profession the then barely known practice of palliative care—a heresy to mainstream medicine bent on delivering cures at ferocious economic and human cost. Saunders had seen how medicine often brutalized patients in order to cure them, and when the so-called cures failed, doctors abandoned patients. When Saunders announced her plan, her mother argued against it: "Medical school at forty-five? You'll be nearly fifty when you graduate." "Mother, dear," she said, "I'll be fifty anyway. Why not also be a doctor?"

Saunders created the first Western hospice—a philosophy of care and an organization to treat those on whom doctors had given up. In a hospice, the sick would not die uncared for or alone, their pain untreated. Saunders's model of allowing patients to dictate their treatment, to gauge their pain and choose their intervention, has changed the paternalistic model of traditional medicine. She founded the modern hospice movement, establishing St. Christopher's in London—a home for the dying that is as spiritual as a church. It was not a *new* thing. Hospices had welcomed sick pilgrims since medieval times. But as a challenge to the medical establishment to face its biases and limits, St. Christopher's captured the *one* thing, an irreducible apprehension about life, which is that no one should die alone or in pain, that death is like childbirth, a passage for which one should be as conscious as necessary. *To find the one thing that may transform others means discovering the irreducible quality in the self.*

That is what this book describes: finding the essential force of one's life story so that one may become inspired to create things so much a part of the human fabric that Time cannot easily erase them; rather Time will become a co-conspirator in keeping them alive, perhaps forever.

In this Art of War with Time, one confronts Time anew. Much like Picasso, the sculptor Louise Nevelson became a greater artist in age than in her youth. She had feared loss of fertility with menopause, but by age fifty-nine, "I had this energy that was flowing like an ocean into creativity. Not fertility but fecundity." Fertility is the condition by which one becomes pregnant. Fecundity means making others pregnant: nourishing, overflowing with grain, wheat, flowers: harvest is maturity. Nevelson's sense of her vitality increased with Time. Instead of making decorative objects as in her youth, she became in her own mind a person who imposes herself on the environment. By defeating Time she conquered Space as well. Her sense of scale expanded. Her built environments became "empires" constructed of "a thousand destructions of the real world." Her mature pieces were walls, structures, half shelters…places that redefined one's experience of space.

• • •

Like Jackie, I found in all of this fecund history one singular source, a Godmother—the mother of all Godmothers. She has survived for over five hundred years looking not a day over thirty. She is ageless, timeless. She is French by citizenship (she resides in the Louvre Museum in Paris) but is Italian by birth—born in Florence in the sixteenth century, the time when Madonnas and the most beautiful women dazzled painters with the simplicity and full power of their presence. In this realm, one painting stands apart. The Mona Lisa is said to be Leonardo da Vinci's essay on immortality. People do not treat her as "only" a painting. Two million visitors travel great distances each year and arrive by the busloads to gaze at her for a few seconds. They have their picture taken with her before the crowd hurries them on. They go away feeling as if they have been blessed. People look at her and feel she looks at them too.

Talk about making an impression. Talk about not becoming invisible in age. Talk about a simple face invested with humility and grandeur. No wonder this face has challenged Time. Of all the paintings in the world, this one dominates. If it is to be read as the great Leonardo's essay on immortality, and the lessons made plain to flesh-and-blood icons like you and me, then we may learn how the artist used this woman to triumph over Time and Space. The Mona Lisa is immortal. She has become a force even though she is but a tiny image on a piece of wood not much larger than a breadbox. She is not beautiful or even pretty. If she were a real live woman, you would not turn your head if you encountered her in the subway. Yet she commands attention. Mona Lisa is a new being, delicate and severe. Distant and minuscule, she has become imprinted on the culture.

Who would not want this iconic power for herself— a force that resides in one's mystery, magic, and authority? What finer pedigree as sources go? What better mirror in which to reflect on one's own image? What more certain guide for how to sit quietly yet command attention, to draw others close for some connection they never lose, even when they turn away?

Leonardo was a student of anatomy and a dreamer who was always experimenting with how to transform one thing into another: lead into gold, bellows into bird wings, and grapeseed oil into a live woman whose eyes follow others around the room, whose flesh looks warm to the touch, and who survives commandingly for over five hundred years.

It is our task to put ourselves into the spirit of this painted icon—she who is the persona of magic because of who she is, not what she does (she doesn't "do" anything). Her presence will become our tutor. We may limn the means by which a painter created a commanding presence that time burnishes.

Leonardo did what no god has yet accomplished: created a woman who ages but remains beautiful—a woman who will not die.

When You Are Old Enough to Believe in Santa

Let us use this painting to tell a new story of age, which unfolds in ten prodigies of mature behavior. Together they form the Stratagem that limns the power of queens and kings, distinct from princes. "Prodigy" is an important word for the talents found in maturity, although it is a term associated with childhood to suggest the outsmarting of Time. A child prodigy may play Mozart at the age of five or beat chess masters with a skill that cannot possibly be the result of her chronological years. A young prodigy may have trouble tying her shoes and yet know the exhilaration of true artistry. So too there are prodigies of maturity—gifts attainable only with age. We mean talents much more exciting than dull "wisdom."

To what ends are the prodigies of maturity useful? As one woman expressed,

> *I want to live to the age of 102 as vital as I am today and upon my death, leave enough assets to pay the tuition of all my grandchildren and of my grieving young husband.*

To arrive at one's mature prodigies, one cannot afford to lose focus, as age sometimes threatens. Without focus, we have no energy. Without energy we attract the sodden and unenergetic: we attract what we put out in the world.

A young woman may mesmerize suitors, soar in her career, become known and admired by strangers. But older women trump the achievements of youth. *They* reduce the glass ceiling to a dust-flecked mirage. *They* win major political elections. *They* are invited into the rarefied realms of institutional power as university presidencies, orchestra conductors, CEOs, and board members—and are welcomed as equals and superiors.

So we may cast a cold eye on youth. We say we want to be young. But do we? A woman's twenties and thirties are not all that great. Our culture has a love-hate relationship with youth. We urge the young to grow up as fast as possible—and then suffer from our unquenchable nostalgia for it.

Youth is a pathology, "Prematurity Syndrome." Youth demands *success*—but it ends up happy with *nonfailure*. The second-rate is lauded; mediocre films and technology and medical care. Artists welcome their maturity because their talent is finally matched by technique. The Renaissance's favorite symbol was the mulberry tree because it flowers late, once every few decades, and then bursts into full bloom. *Make haste slowly* was Leonardo's motto. He valued the long gestation—works, ideas, passions that burst into life as if fully born and alive.

Masterpieces have this quality, whether Elizabeth I's England, or Abigail Adams's co-presidency with her husband John; or anthropologist Jane Goodall's rebirth from a clone of her mentor, the anthropologist Louis Leakey, to a creative force all her own in the study of animal behavior and preservation, or Katharine Graham's late-life re-creation from an emotionally abused housewife to an internationally celebrated newspaper publisher who made the press a force that politicians had to fear and respect. Or Leonardo's Mona. Such are the prodigies of maturity. Such women redefine Time to their own ends rather than allow it to defeat them. For example, to an aficionado of long gestations, "writer's block" would instead be seen as "thinker's flow." Marilynne Robinson's Pulitzer Prize–winning novel *Gilead* was twenty-four years not in the making but in the thinking...that is the kind of new timing that youth and development models do not value, but the efforts of maturity do. A long runway means a high takeoff.

Onward the Laws of Backwards Time

On the other hand, why should we make an effort to mature when all around us maturity is confused with the loss of beauty and power? Greta Garbo went into hiding before she was forty. Goldie Hawn, in her sixties, plays abandoned wives. Germaine Greer preaches that a real woman's sexual liberation is liberation from sex. These are fears of age. How different things look when you really study how Time changes as you cross the barrier of age forty-five.

Know how when you cross the equator, winter is summer and the toilets supposedly flush counterclockwise? Cross the equatorial age line of forty-five or fifty and the laws of nature change—giving mature women a new primacy. Here is the first law of counterclockwise Time and über-femininity:

When a mature woman seduces a man, he *becomes pregnant, not she.*

A man could not have this power over another man. Nor could a young woman possess anything like this force. A mature woman makes others pregnant with ideas, mysteries, freedom, playfulness. And not just one man. She has the potential to have as strong an impact on one man or a hundred, one woman or a crowd, in all arenas: intimate, social, and political.

The laws of counterclockwise Time allow us to discard the fantasy or mask of femininity for the reality behind it.

The second law of counterclockwise Time and the new/old femininity is this:

By fifty a woman is praised for what she had been blamed for.

Emily Dickinson received her first marriage proposal and wrote the best poems of her life after age fifty, including letters that are among the most beautiful in literature and give the lie to the image of the recluse of Amherst. Her reclusive ways turned into exclusive ways. Her power was exerted upon a chosen few. Georgia O'Keeffe emerged from the shadows as husband Alfred Stieglitz's muse to create an art in her own idiom, in her own high desert home, Ghost Ranch in New Mexico, at age forty-seven. Internationally celebrated, O'Keeffe too retreated but kept attention upon her creative work. Florence Nightingale invented the

British sewer system and the nursing profession from her bed after a youth spent aiding soldiers injured in the Crimean War. Her power too resided in a different and self-created arena of power.

Madeleine Albright did not believe she could be chosen secretary of state. She was sure her stubbornness and opinions would stand in her way—but by the time she was sixty, these seemed to her and to President Bill Clinton to be strengths, not weaknesses. The novelist Edith Wharton had her first orgasm at age forty-five. Colette wrote her first book under her own name at age fifty, and at sixty-two found true love with a young man nearly half her age. Isak Dinesen, pen name for Karen Blixen, the author of *Out of Africa*, was in her late forties when she began writing professionally. She never believed she had been born an artist, but grief over having lost her farm and her lover in Africa made her a writer and gave her a second life. The architect Zaha Hadid was everyone's personal Alfred Hitchcock movie for twenty years: she would get contracts to build something big but invariably lose them, leaving her fans in unbearable suspense. Finally at fifty-three, she won the international Pritzker Prize and her reputation was assured.

Hadid won because designs considered odd coming from a young woman seemed fascinating coming from an oracular older woman. Shapes of buildings as odd as pasta or bridges as futuristic as wormholes were no longer seen as bizarre and threatening. Authored by a woman of age, they were considered part of tradition, not unsauced penne but ingeniously borne structures hallowed by ancient Roman influences and Baroque spirals. Time had declared a truce with Hadid. Or perhaps she had wrestled Time to a truce. Finally she did not seem special—read *weird*—but a visionary with a genius for history. She became a counterclockwise law unto herself.

Someday we will be mature enough to understand what is in O'Keeffe's desert imagery, in Dickinson's silent dashes that thread through her poems, in Albright's brilliant flowering, in Saunders's determined action that had the forcefulness of prayer, in Wharton's submission to another person at an age when she was finally in control of her destiny, in Dinesen's full recovery from a wrecked youthful marriage to a practice of loving the world, and in Hadid's being acknowledged, finally, for innovations others had ripped off from her.

Everything we know about human satisfaction focuses on a model of development, on evolving or progressing. This alters our sense of Time so that the next thing is more appealing than what we already have. No wonder that just as we get what we crave, it appears hollow, a mere transition to the next plateau. A model of human arrival—not development—would acknowledge that it is the finish that make us happiest. Mature women are like wine: grapes transfigured into spirit. As in wine, the finish counts. A moviegoer may hate two-thirds of a film, psychologists find, but praise it if it ends brilliantly. Finishes are the peaks of experience. *We have finally become the person we had wanted to be . . . perhaps the person we are destined to be.*

Here is the third law of counterclockwise Time as it benefits femininity:

In age, a woman can be younger than she ever was.

The third law is the most exciting, because when we admit its truth, we know that Time has a minimal hold over us. This law actually allows us to travel through Time as if it were a country. We detect in ourselves:

- a rebellious spark expressed as a going against whatever is new and current;
- submission as a form of self-mastery (also experienced as an unproductive productivity)— submission to pleasure and optimism;
- a desire to give and receive unconditional love. Romantic love turns out to be an illusion. But unconditional love turns out to be completely possible. Mature, we realize that there is something more important than survival: it is love.

A true Time Warrior thrives under these laws and uses them to become a force equal to Time. George Eliot took a rebellious creative leap when she stopped editing other people's books and began writing her own. She wrote a masterpiece, *Middlemarch*, at age forty-five. At age forty-seven, in 1845, she wrote her second masterpiece, *Daniel Deronda*. She was helped by two men who loved her unconditionally at the same time from her forty-fifth year onward: her publisher John Blackwood and her life partner, George Henry Lewes. They thought the novel *Daniel Deronda* too strange, too bold and innovative and a going against the times, to be a popular success, but each dedicated himself to assuring she would complete it. Her thanks to these two was unstinting. When Lewes died, she felt half dead, yet there remained a rebellious spark of life in her. She talks then about submitting to life more than ever. *With submission comes self-mastery of a large and generous and experimental sort.* Soon after Lewes's death, she married young John Cross and died seven months later, at a peak of happiness.

> *Youth can never achieve anything. What can one enjoy at thirty? Young, you can't pick fruit from the tree you planted. You've had no time for joy or thought. You are more like a tortoise or a raven, living a bare animal existence: eating, sleeping, and procreating. But if you*

have years after youth, time in which to become a master—then you have everything life offers.

So wrote Karel Capek in a play, a parable in which a woman remains forty-five years old for several hundred years. The young envy her, the old admire her, and everyone craves her secret. But when her admirers gain possession of it, one young woman, threatened by the power of maturity, burns the paper upon which it is written, losing it forever.

Or did she merely destroy it for a time? The lost formula reappears in the actions of the women described in this book.

"At age sixty-eight I'm every age I ever was. I always think that I'm not just sixty-eight. I'm also fifty-five and twenty-one and three. Oh, especially three." George Carlin said that. Cross the equatorial age line and recognize that maturity consists of all the ages you ever were.

Young, we learn to say what we think, forcefully, directly. But when you are fifty-five and twenty-one and three, to be heard is to speak with one voice that carries the range of all these ages.

How to Use This Book

A warrior against Time has no lesser enemies. No one else, nothing else, daunts her. There is no force so invisible and destructive but also as giving and occasionally forgiving as Time—after all, we cannot live but in Time. Stand up to Time and you gain tremendous strength of character. The ten tactics of the Stratagem enable you to do this. They are culled from the examples of the great women of history and reveal the practices of mirroring, positioning, rhetoric, seriousness, and organization building that characterize the second half or second third of life.

Power resides in the ability to make oneself an icon, to be seen and heard in ways that are entirely different from youthful ways. This is a book about how to arrest Time for a time.

The tactics may be followed in no particular order. If, however, you follow these practices in the sequence laid out here, you learn how the great women of history have advanced from maturity itself to a focused power of maturity: a commanding beauty—a presence that exerts a powerful force upon others. You will find the means by which age will make you stronger. You will be able to do more with less exertion; your presence alone will accomplish more than all the actions of the young. You will see how to persist or to make a comeback.

The Mona Lisa is your true north. All the tactics find their basic expression in her. She is icon and exemplar; to keep her in mind is to have the whole Stratagem in one vision. *What you behold you shall become.* Leonardo's enduring image is the reminder of how to arrest Time.

No wonder that this work is the most memorable to billions of people and has survived for so long.

Women, *age*, and *power*: these are the elements of our magic formula. But the crucial fourth element is *strategy*. The kingdoms of the earth are in social turmoil and political turmoil. Only strategy—or plotting against one's weaknesses and others'—will allow a woman to restore her pleasure, revive her energy, and transfer power to others. Only a singular stratagem by which we may mature as quickly as possible will save us from ruin by the young yahoos and the Lords of the Flies.

Practicing a strategy makes us attentive and intentional. If we do not take full responsibility for what we are or for what any given situation demands of us, then we grow weak. We lose a piece of ourselves. The next time our attention wanders at a critical moment and we cannot rise to the occasion, we lose a chance to reach the goal.

When maturity is valued by *all* people, it will recover its necessary place in the realms of intimacy and world politics. Then the stratagem will have worked and this book will need never be read again.

The Stratagem

AGELESS AND TIMELESS IN TEN TACTICS

TACTIC 1

Only the woman who has faced enormous loss may proclaim herself first among the immortals, because she is invulnerable to the wounds inflicted by mere humans.

To stand up to Time requires art more than battle. But only a certain kind of art will do. There is no point in fighting Time with a surgeon's knife: this turns a real person into a plastic rose. And not all the long-lived are expert advisors: there are no lessons to be learned from ancient Rome. Age and weariness—Time's assassins—defeated the Romans at their civilization's most mature as no marauder or routine enemy could.

Time ruins more civilizations and personal dreams than all other forces combined. Between now and the moment Leonardo finished his work on the Mona Lisa in 1503, countries have fallen and arisen, people have disappeared into oblivion. Throughout Time, *she* remains grinning.

To "read" Leonardo's essay on immortality that is the Mona Lisa, to see in your soul what the great painter saw in his—this is our purpose. We seek the masterpiece inside the masterpiece, the human equivalent of an immortal work of art. Let us now understand the nature of our struggle and find the figure inside of us that commands Time and waits for maturity to reveal itself.

• • •

All men and women fear Time. When we are young, Time flexes its power over us with a benign force. It moves with a soothing, rocking repetition. We wake every day and feed the baby, cuddle the spouse, repeat the job. The days march on. We conform our lives to calendars and schedules. And then suddenly Time turns cruel. We can no longer schedule it into submission; it moves too fast. We try to outrun Time by deceiving ourselves, claiming that fifty is the new forty when it is, honestly, fifty. By such deceptions our personal empires crumble.

> The walls of Time and Space are real only to those who have given up on life. You have more power over Time than you know.

Time is a mighty enemy. We cannot deceive ourselves of that. But you are a mighty force. The health and success of a human life has a great deal to do with its correspondence to its time. A good and true sense of timing can win a person a raise, ensure that a story or a joke is well told, and open the heart to falling in love with the right person "at the right time."

How might you become a force equal to Time? By imagining that life is eternal. For if that is our belief, as the nineteenth-century writer Aurore Dupin, renamed George Sand, said, then

> let us run our course bravely. If it's otherwise and the self perishes completely, let's earn the honor of having performed our task, our duty—for we have no clear duties but towards ourselves and our fellow-creatures. WHAT WE DESTROY IN OURSELVES WE DESTROY IN THEM. Our abasement degrades them, our falls drag them down; we owe it to them to remain upright so that they may not be laid low.

We already know something about how to conquer Time. We have the power to draw out moments to derive intense happiness from them. We make people forget a second or an hour is passing when we speak compellingly or act with intimacy. We make Time irrelevent. When we walk into a room, we may draw all eyes to us as if nothing else were happening anywhere in the world—as if Time has stopped upon our arrival. That is a quality which defangs ferocious Time. That is a kind of heroism which equals any. To beguile Time is to outdo nature's toughest general. With this simple assurance, we may begin the Stratagem.

The Surest Route to Disaster Is Misperceiving Your True Strength

All of the guides to power—the arts of war and strategy—equate power with youth. Yet each stage of life requires a different heroism—a new stratagem. For the young, physical beauty is a form of heroism. Youth attracts attention and conquers hearts easily. Yet that kind of instant force loses its thrill. Not everything you want to do can be accomplished through youthful seduction. And so a heroine eventually learns aggression: she competes, she negotiates, and by such means she becomes another kind of heroine. Eventually accomplishment gained by the show of such dominance also grows boring and success as a goal grows pale. The need for happiness, pleasure, and comfort for oneself and others becomes preeminent: that is the first blush of maturity. And believe it or not, satisfying even those needs eventually becomes dull. When that happens, one has arrived at the peak of maturity. It is a scary mountaintop.

A heroine then has less of a future to plan, and her

past too seems distant and irrelevant. One becomes then like a beggar with an empty begging bowl out on a journey to find God or the meaning of one's life. That is the last heroic quest we take on. Heroism at that stage requires living entirely in the moment, for only the moment provides us with feelings of depth, rest, and also purpose. Life's heroic path winds up requiring the opposite of the heroic qualities of youth. We end up having to learn the value of submission instead of defiance, indelible friendship as equal to love, and devotion as bringing us more delights than desire may deliver.

Maturity *is* the mountaintop. At that height, we face a choice: to retire from the center of action or to conduct our lives differently. If we withdraw from constant work, we risk drifting into isolation, watching TV alone and counting the minutes until dinner. However, if we recommit to a goal, we must be careful not to rewarm some old ambition. We ought to finally yield to a pursuit we have been waiting decades for the freedom and confidence to accomplish.

Time seasons a woman for a significant heroism slowly. Joan of Arc tried her all and died at seventeen. Simone Weil, the brilliant French martyr, died at thirty-four on a hunger strike to resist France's collaboration with the Nazis. Sylvia Plath fought her demons until she couldn't fight them anymore and killed herself at age thirty. The list of young heroines who spend themselves all at once or early on is long and sad. Machiavelli wrote a whole book advising a prince to fight and conquer with youthful abandon. Princessas, as we may call such feminine counterparts, are similarly carpe-diem gals: they must get that raise or someone else will; they must outshine and outsmart a nasty colleague, and do so immediately and dramatically. They must grab the spotlight, otherwise the opportunity will have passed. Quick changes and immediate gain to a prince or a princessa are everything, a clear sign of triumph.

But after a certain age, one isn't a princessa anymore. One does not fight conventional enemies any longer. One doesn't even fight to win. One princessa recounted how, at age fifty, she fought her husband's doctors against his dismal prognosis. She used the same tactics of besting or outsmarting opponents. These had helped her reverse deprivations in her youth and had enabled her to succeed in her job and thrive in her relationships. But instead of helping her sick husband, her inspired willfulness and her commitment to changing outcomes made his suffering worse. She put him through endless trials and experiments, and put herself through clever but pointless arguments with his doctors. She blinded herself to reality, living on hope, which is, as Shakespeare said, a great breakfast but a bad supper. Princessas are brilliant at reconfiguring reality to meet their young or early expectations of life. But in maturity, the goals are different and the means to achieving them are different too.

The Art of a Long Life Is the Art of Loving Loss

Princessas' techniques draw upon a youthful femininity much as *The Prince*'s techniques draw upon adolescent spunk to conquer all. Princessas use tears to break through opposition. They also act as spies, studying people's motives so they might appeal to the better angels of their natures.

By such means, a young woman may indeed change her fate. "Ask for everything," the princessa is advised: because if you have little and are ambitious for much, asking for everything makes you seem in others' eyes as if you are worthy of a raise, a promotion, or support for your idea. But ask for everything when you already have a wealth of mature experience, and you get what you *don't* need. Opportunities that don't last. Endless changes. Confusion.

Princes and princessas strategize for gain. They insist the world give them their full due: victory at the end of battle. But the power axis reverses in maturity. The new heroism is in loss. Knowing this, the mature take on the character of Time itself: Time, the thief. The successful warrior always uses the enemy's weapons against the enemy. We submit to loss as evidence of our strength.

Loss is feminine heroism. Myth teaches us that boys become men by a stratagem of acquisition: they build strength, amass arms, and then go out and slay a dragon, fight a war, or win a competition. By such deeds they acquire a reputation, and with it money that leads to wealth, admiration that builds to love, and alliances that expand into whole kingdoms. In maturity, their heroic reputation spreads. Their stature is based on tales of increase.

Women's lives follow exactly the opposite path. Girls start out with everything they need: they are fertile; they have the means and strength to bear life, to raise and tend families. Every day they sacrifice themselves, not just once or twice in battle. They spend their wealth and health constantly. Their lives are not marked by gain. Their children leave home, spouses may grow bored and distant, youthful beauty departs, and career opportunities decline. The years bring one loss after another.

By the traditional measure of heroism, women's lives are marked by loss. But by a different measure, Time actually reduces a woman to her essence, her heroic self. She burns down to the bone, to her irreducible essence, her most forceful, concentrated character—qualities virtually impervious to Time's further larcenies. She then has at her command new powers.

Loss is not the cause for tears, it is "honey," Emily

Dickinson insisted. "Beloved Shakespeare says, 'He that is robbed and smiles, steals something from the thief.'" She writes this shortly after the death of her late-life lover, Judge Lord, who proposed marriage to her.

She says of George Eliot, Mary Ann Evans, whose writing she admires: her life is "a doom of fruit without the bloom":

> *Her losses make our gains ashamed—*
> *She bore life's empty pack*
> *As gallantly as if the East*
> *Were swinging at her back.*
> *Life's empty pack is heaviest,*
> *As every porter knows—*
> *In vain to punish honey,*
> *It only sweeter grows.*

Qualities that resist Time and aging have been coveted by men who are seekers of truth. It is why Odysseus abandoned the seductive young Calypso to return home to his aging wife, Penelope, spurred on by his undying love for her. It inspired the poet Dante to make a dangerous journey to the immortal Beatrice, to prove himself worthy of being schooled by her in the feminine mysteries, the mystery of eternity.

Loss restores a person to a state of essential femininity.

We war with Time but we do not win against Time. In-

stead, we give up the notion of winning and of acquiring even more. Our power is in submitting to our losses, and finding new opportunities in doing so.

•   •   •

I knew none of this when I wrote *The Princessa: Machiavelli for Women* in 1997. That little bullet of a book was a woman's version of *The Prince*, the classic Renaissance analysis of the strategy that brought princes to power, now standard reading for managers, salesmen, politicians, and graduates of the U.S. Army's elite Delta Force. *The Prince* maintains that one is more successful if one is feared rather than loved; it defines power as domination. *The Princessa*, a study of how women have prevailed throughout history despite the odds against them, also insisted that women become more strategic to achieve the rewards they are due. But in place of fear, *The Princessa* promoted the potency of love to turn the toughest situations to a woman's favor. I assumed that the lessons of power, once learned, may easily be repeated as necessary throughout one's lifetime.

But as a young and immature woman, I did not appreciate the threat of Time. I did not see that the art of female power must change, because the nature of femininity changes so dramatically after age forty-five.

Consider a heroine described in *The Princessa*, the ancient Sumerian princess Inanna. She had attained her throne by "besting" her own father, coyly stealing the gifts of civilization he hoarded for himself and then liberating them for all to enjoy. "Besting" or surprising an opponent is a key princessa tactic.

Case closed, I thought. However, Inanna was to be called to true courage later. She reached an age where she plunged into depression, no longer able to enjoy the power of her youthful beauty; deprived of the certainty of her judgments; underwhelmed by her high office and past achievements. Inanna's anxiety may best be characterized by Count Leo Tolstoy, who plunged into the same spiral of loss:

> I was sure that something had broken within me on which my life had always rested, and that I had nothing left to hold on to, and that morally my life had stopped. An invincible force impelled me to get rid of my existence in one way or another. It cannot be said that I wished to kill myself, for the force which drew me away from life was fuller, more powerful, more general than any mere desire. It was a force like my old aspiration to live, only it impelled me in the opposite direction.

An empowered sense of life begins when we beg fate for new gifts to escape the pattern of confusion or loss, depression, and pain that accumulates in the late forties.

Inanna felt like a corpse. She once considered herself

"special" but not anymore. She saw herself as dust, and like everyone, to dust she would return. To experience the human condition began to excite her as her throne once did. This new connection with humankind gave her the impetus to start her life anew. According to the tale, she exits the Kingdom of the Dead—her depression—"naked and bowed low." Humble. Naked and bowed low is the position in which babies are born. Naked and bowed by loss, Inanna is befriended by a lowly fly, a buzzing creature more fit for the wine vats of her ancient town of Sumer than for associating with this royal woman. An inebriated little fly buzzing in comical circles leads her back home, or in the language of the myth, leads her from a youth of sacrifice and seriousness to a profound and spiritual ecstasy. (The first followers of the god of wine, Dionysus, were mature women who were exuberant. They never imbibed the gods' spirits; but they associated themselves with his spirit of optimism.)

The fly leads Inanna to a new life in her own home. As a princessa, she discovered the civilizing gifts. As a mature woman, she discovers *her own buried nature* in the riches of being human. She sees this as true royalty.

The new heroine confronts Enemy Time by confronting loss as an artist discovers it, in the elements of a human life reduced to its essential nature, beyond even character, to a nature that is not special, personal, or individual, but highly typical. Not even deserving of special treatment, but rather all too human, Inanna, mature, is no longer special and apart. She has gone from "I" to "we."

If loss is the ground upon which a woman comes into her strength, how may she fight Time or at least trick it, slow it, make it do her bidding?

There Are Two Ways to Be *Erotic*: to Cover Up or to Show Oneself. But to Be *Magic* Is to Do Both

A woman of mature power positions herself somewhere between psychology and myth, or between being known and being mysterious, her mind revealed yet her soul distant, impossible to comprehend. This quality is the essence of the Mona Lisa, as captured by the most famous words ever written about a painting. These words contain the clue to how a woman may increase her stature through loss of individuality:

> *The presence that rose thus so strangely beside the waters, is expressive of what in the ways of a thousand years men had come to desire. Hers is the head upon which all "the ends of the world are come," and the eyelids are a little weary. It is a beauty wrought out from within upon the flesh, the deposit, little cell by cell, of strange thoughts and fantastic reveries and exquisite passions. Set it for a moment beside one of those*

white Greek goddesses or beautiful women of antiquity, and how would they be troubled by this beauty, into which the soul with all its maladies has passed! All the thoughts and experience of the world have etched and molded there, in that which they have of power to refine and make expressive the outward form, the animalism of Greece, the lust of Rome, the mysticism of the middle age with its spiritual ambition and imaginative loves, the return of the Pagan world, the sins of the Borgias. She is older than the rocks among which she sits; like the vampire, she has been dead many times, and learned the secrets of the grave; and has been a diver in deep seas, and keeps their fallen day about her; and trafficked for strange webs with Eastern merchants: and, as Leda, was the mother of Helen of Troy, and, as Saint Anne, the mother of Mary; and all this has been to her but as the sound of lyres and flutes, and lives only in the delicacy with which it has molded the changing lineaments, and tinged the eyelids and the hands. The fancy of a perpetual life, sweeping together ten thousand experiences, is an old one; and modern philosophy has conceived the idea of humanity as wrought upon by, and summing up in itself, all modes of thought and life. Certainly Lady Lisa might stand as the embodiment of the old fancy, the symbol of the modern idea.

This is the image of a woman sitting as if upon a throne: observers look up at her. But her throne is commonplace: over both her shoulders are modest and almost spiritual landscapes. She maintains a distance. One never knows what she is thinking, and when one tries to guess, Walter Pater tells us, we sense the figure before us is not one woman but is a reflection of many faces and many epochs. She is born an "I" but becomes a "we"—all women. She is a time traveler, too. She is young, old, eternal. Vampire, diver into seas so deep they drink down Time, she enjoys the fancy of a perpetual life and ten thousand existences. Time doesn't cramp her style. Her story always ends happily. She is liberated from Time. She is not thirty or one hundred or five hundred years old. She has longevity not bound by age-counts. She outlives her own life.

The way in which one penetrates the face of Mona Lisa until one finally expresses the mystery of creation itself is very similar to the way a woman penetrates her own power. At first glance, one sees in the magic mirror of the canvas a strangely beautiful woman. Then one peers in closer and sees more unfamiliar faces...a sense not that an individual is looking back at you, but womanhood in all its power. This is what we gain by our losses—the bedrock of femininity. How do we lose the personality we worked so hard to create but now is the prison of our youth? I tell people that I spent half my life creating "Harriet Rubin," and now I want to disown her. She is too small a creature for the pleasures of maturity.

The painting, says Pater, is a record of a woman's life as Woman. *The mature face is iconic or bears the marks of many souls—the state of extreme femininity rather than particular individuality.* Maturity demands we loosen our identification with our individual past, our problematic parents, our youthful glories or mistakes. To become iconic is to gain a new prodigy or talent: *the genius of history*, whereby we recognize we are an entire history.

Maturity judges itself not by an individual past—but by the *past*: by women who made their mark upon history. The faces of immortal women—Helen, Greek statuary, Mary's mother, Elizabeth—are in Mona Lisa's. The mature will feel judged by *their* standards. A woman may not feel that they are exceptional and she is not. She will develop a consciousness of them throughout the career of her life, whose goal is pleasure more than narrow success or nonfailure. The qualities of this mind are more important than her own private mind. In the same way, a poet who aspires to be great will acknowledge his debt to Homer and Shakespeare and dozens of others.

A warrior against Time thinks of herself as an icon:

this is the face of individual loss, the face of the eternal feminine.

She thinks of herself as being an icon, an icon being like a visual cell phone from beyond: people don't look at you, rather they receive you—a message that is like a healing force or image—and they respond. An icon is a healing presence. People may fear an iconic image's forcefulness, much as early Christians rubbed the eyes out from images of a woman named Tecla so that she would not stare at the viewer and command power over him. To enlighten (or arouse) a person by meeting their gaze, by one's presence or being, is an icon's power.

Look into the eyes of an icon and know its power to transform. The ancient prophets warned: *you become what you behold.* To study Leonardo's painting, to look into the magic mirror that is the Mona Lisa, is become iconic, to come to imitate the look by which a face defies Time.

• • •

Time is a painter too, as great as Leonardo. Age redraws our face. The tight individualized features of youth soften or vanish. Age hollows or rounds out the cheeks, narrows the lips often to a simple slash across the face, gives the nose prominence. As the traits of individuality erode on the surface of the face, so too are they abraded in our sense of ourselves. George Sand says of her own mental transformation to match her facial changes that she becomes less herself and more womanly:

> *I find it quite hard to find the "I" that once interested me, and which I've started to address as "you" in the plural.*

Thinking of oneself as *we* becomes a source of strength, a figure of the eternal feminine. The first and fundamental loss is a source more powerful than realizing our personalities as Jane or Julie or John. "Ever more calm [is] beginning to reign in my once agitated soul," Sand said:

> *My brain proceeds only from synthesis to analysis now; before it used to do the opposite. What presents itself to me now when I wake up in the morning is the world as a whole.*

So we begin the Stratagem by looking deeply into the Mona Lisa as our magic mirror. Better than any cold glass, it reflects back our mystery, not our flaws. Upon that we shall concentrate. Gaze at the Mona Lisa and your lips will form her mysterious smile, your glance will soften, your body will mimic her beckoning, *contraposto* position, turned slightly toward you, slightly away. Nothing about this portrait is accidental. Not the use of shadow applied so that, when your glance moves away from her mouth, she starts to frown as if she were alive. Not the fact that her hair is painted in brushstrokes common to depictions of rivers, symbols of endless life. Not the fact that the latticework on her bodice is the artist's signature: *vinci* means "lattice." Even that pose, when you take it out of the painting and into real life and sit in such a way, draws others to lean closer to you, as if you were about to leave in the next minute, and their desire is to make you stay. Let us become her.

The Mona Lisa was the only one of Leonardo's paintings to be with the artist when he died on May 2, 1519, in the palace of King François I of France. Such was the speculation of what the painting *might* depict—the essence of its great creator—that the king planned to watch as the great master's soul left the artist's body and made its way to heaven. He wished to know if indeed that odd masculine and feminine face depicted was the image Leonardo saw when looking into his own soul—his own mirror. For a person to recognize her own soul is a triumph. As Socrates bids us all, "Know thyself." But for a person, even a king, to see the great Leonardo's soul, that is a rare opportunity.

The king, to his dismay, arrived moments after Leonardo's passing. Believing that Leonardo's undying genius was in the Mona Lisa's face, François bought the painting and hung it in his privy, where he and the timeless iconic woman could be alone together. The Louvre is built upon the site of the king's bathroom.

Art teaches us to see "something outside ourselves that is higher than what is within us, and gradually, through contemplation and admiration, to come to resemble it."

Art, then, is our "second opinion" on aging—our resource in fighting Time. It alone can revise not only the way we look but something more radical: the way in which we allow ourselves to be seen.

TACTIC 2

In any situation in which you wish
to be treated royally, be yourself, and
others will play "the queen."

To become a queen of your domain, to win the recognition for which your experience and intelligence now qualify you, to attain the loves you deserve and to find the means to enact the most auspicious social changes, prepare so well for battle that battle is rendered unnecessary. Effectiveness grows with your submission to Time, not with extravagant displays of force, compromise, or sacrifice. Not, in other words, with trying to do more just to tread water against Time.

Pass through the curtain of effort and endless struggle into the majesty of being. The relaxation of effort buys you more. As Lily Tomlin said, "In age one becomes less physical and more metaphysical." Consider how one woman enacted this: The woman, a modern actress, wished to play the role of Queen Elizabeth I, perhaps the greatest female monarch who ever lived and a true Renaissance ruler; yet the actress kept failing at the task. Elizabeth built a global British empire that her most brilliant subject, Shakespeare, immortalized; she built it from a monarchy of dust she inherited from her cruel father, Henry VIII, who beheaded her own mother. The actress, at fifty, could not summon the confidence intrinsic to a ruler who loved her people and expected to be loved in return. She tried the conventional power ploys: she raised her voice and spoke insistently. When that did not elicit respect, she became subdued to lure others in close to listen. But this theater of leadership is not what the Stratagem requires. The dramatics of Princessas—flattery, tears, tons of requests made of others—does not work for those who have a wealth of power already. The Stratagem allows one to create more by doing less. To sit quietly, like the Mona Lisa herself, and draw others close requires a level of intention that pulls others to you with intense fascination. Radiate a calm, clear intent and you have and hold authority without exerting it. To be seen as powerful requires, in maturity, doing less and representing or embodying more.

What does this mean? The director solved the puzzle for the struggling actress in these words: "Be yourself, and others will play 'the queen.' " *Others* play *the queen*? He meant for the actress to put herself first in her own estimation. She was to get over self-doubt. She was to expect good things to come to her, whether or not she deserved them. Her presence alone would enhance others. "What happens," Isak Dinesen wrote, "happens because it pleases the Queen."

Modern times define the feminine merely as the flirtatious, which limits the voice of femininity to the key of youth. Yet true femininity is stylistically more akin to parental strength, deriving from images of "the Great Mother," which we know as Mother Nature or the office of "queen," or the Virgin Mary. The actress in question had to reach beyond contemporary and immature or unripe versions of femininity. To be herself, a queen is not just a woman with a specific history, but the very essence of a powerful female. Her power is her femininity: a stand for justice, love, and commitment to doing what is right and best and most compelling: to be the embodiment of the creative force that bears and destroys. A big maternal force contains everything, and to recognize that capacity in oneself prompts others to step back and be grateful to be in the midst of the queen. A person with the power of intention draws others to her. Intention is more important than invention, which was a habit of youth that needs the ever-new-like toys to keep itself occupied.

Intention is a kind of centering that puts oneself at the center, but as a source, not as a subject, like the sun. One of the greatest leaders of all time, a celibate Indian doctor reached the United States at age sixty-two in his first trip abroad. He was dead tired, but when the Bangladeshi chambermaid arrived in his hotel room for the turn-down service, he detained her in conversation for as long as he could. The handler who went to check on him thought he was making a mere show of interest in the maid, the benevolence a Brahmin graciously extends to a person of a lower caste. That was not the case at all. He was inquiring with steady persistence how she had learned to clean rooms without knowing English, without any degree of literacy at all. He wanted to learn from her how to create training programs at his hospital for the poor in southern India, programs so flawlessly simple that they could be taught to illiterate workers who would then find paid employment for the first time in their lives. He did not look for opportunities; they came to him because he knew his purpose as a being meant to create peace, compassion, and a sense that the fundament of the world was love and creation.

To embody such intentionality is to be immune to fatigue too. When we are fully engaged, we do not need sleep. Or rather, we are at rest even when excited, like monks who in the most intense periods of wakeful meditation slow their heart rate to a calm beat.

Elizabeth's own intentionality was created by giving away none of her power to men, to children, to subjects. She considered herself to be doing God's work. To be convinced of oneself as a person of consequence goes beyond sacrificing oneself for another or a task.

One's primary ground of meaning in age moves from the body to the soul. A woman who discovers her power late becomes more spiritually and symbolically feminine, more womanly, not less. She acquires an iconic presence—a form of power that history calls a second body or subtle body, a presence filled with promise.

Every great woman has this iconic quality. One notices it immediately in aspects of spiritual seduction. Of Eleanor Roosevelt it was said that she was a light. Of Julia Child, that she resembled "a great big tree" not only because of her height of six feet but because so many apprentice chefs felt they could find generosity or shelter in her laugh and in her devotion to cooking as an art. Of the architect Zaha Hadid, that she reminds clients of Cleopatra, all earthly majesty. Of Elizabeth I, history recalls that she deliberately, even calculatingly, evoked the goddess of diplomacy and peace, Astrea, down to her dress and gestures and speech. Of the Mona Lisa herself, it is said that she conveys the mystery of the Sphinx. This is using one's mystery to capture attention and hold it. A presence is entirely mysterious and is more attractive than any conventional beauty.

We are speaking not about literal appearance, though we soon shall speak of the quality of facial heraldry to which this spirituality gives visibility. However, all great women have the undersong of the Leonardo portrait: the suggestion that just beyond the nose or jawline or smile is a tradition of which we are the full representative. To yield our sense of individuality, even personality, to representing this universal quality is to embody this source of strength. Our tradition and highest office is the quality of the ultra-feminine, and it does not age. *True femininity is ageless and eternal.* When we let this tradition flood us, we are more. When we enter a meeting or join a party, people have an immediate impression or feeling about us. Something mysterious beyond our individual physical presence attracts attention. We remind observers of something, some big story of life, mystery, or the importance of female ways. We give off an energy or image beyond our literal appearance. We do this naturally. But only if we are aware of this iconic force do we *remain* in the observer's consciousness. We do not then arrive as if we had just gotten out of a taxi but out of some tale.

When others play "the queen," they are deferring to the second body. This belief that kings and queens were immortal the more they were a type and not a mere individual arose in the Middle Ages, when theorists of power were more aware of the effects of subtle forces upon the psyche. These forces still exist, only our awareness of how to use them has dimmed.

Our second body does not die, and it is not our personal property stamped with our individual nature, like our soul. It is our immortal presence as woman: the über-feminine self that resists Time's grasp.

And so we encourage others to play the queen. The actress who was to play Elizabeth I learned to speak her lines as if independent of others' opinions and completely invested in her own, not egotistically but *as representative of her subjects, not beholden to their opinions of her.* Her centripetal force drew others. She came to believe that the occupations of her own mind were not frivolously personal or eccentric but broadly practical. She saw herself as being of dynastic importance, standing in the line of a history of women who set out to have an impact, and thought that everything she touched in her personal life would have ongoing social or political ramifications.

Long-lived Queens Have "a Genius for History" as Creators of the Future, Not Mere Consumers of It

Power at its essence is an animal quality. It exerts a force beyond reason or effort. It resides in a quality of being an exquisite *type*.

Consider a cat on a stage whose eyes are following a piece of lint that floats on the breeze. The cat will command the audience's attention no matter how dramatic the human action is elsewhere onstage. An animal will always upstage a human being because it is completely and authentically itself: its feline nature is to the cat what the expression of femininity is to a woman. The more a woman expresses typical female qualities, the greater her mystery and the greater her command.

A cat—like a queen—has two bodies: one is mortal and physical, the other is iconic. The second body is what we speak of as "nine lives." It is the iconic "cat." Its second self is ageless and timeless. All who love cats are fascinated by their undying iconic quality: their individuality and the typicalness of their kind. When it is said that "the queen is dead, long live the queen," the reference is to this symbolic presence—the essence of eternal femininity. It is the drama of loss *and* restoration, submission to fate and Time but also to power over them. Think of how wine is the second but best self of grapes and Camembert is the second and most complete embodiment of young insipid cream. Cream is sweet, but only Camembert has earned the intensity to be nicknamed "the feet of the goddess." To kiss these feet is to taste heaven.

This second self is the matured and eternal self. This is the aspect of the self that holds its own in memory.

To take on the qualities of this second body in our mortal years is to acquire the properties of ripeness, which makes age the years of glory and power. It is the way to grow equal to Time.

The reigning monarch was thought to have an immortal body. When a woman ripens into a full expression of femininity, she may age, weaken, even disappoint, but there will always be something about her that is impervious to Time.

In the Middle Ages, the queen's second body was believed to be a link between God or the gods and the people whom she governed: her nature an element between psychology and myth. So powerful was this second self, in fact, that the happiness of the queen was said to be directly tied to her subjects'. If the queen was sad, it was thought that the earth would grow fallow, laws would subside into chaos, and disharmony would fill the land and corrupt people's hearts.

Part of the queen therefore borrowed from the Kingdom of the Mothers the idea of Mother Nature, which is a whole different sense of Time than we measure by the clock. The world of the Mothers considers progress a myth with which we console ourselves. The matrix of the Mothers is governed by repetition and deepening of instinct, by expanding circles of friendship, not competition, and by a belief that the best is never found in the new-new but in the unalterable qualities of tradition. Time moves in circles, not in a straight path.

Storytellers live in this time; so many of our examples of queenly behavior derive from the world of artists and their authorial voices. Storytellers have a strong link to their symbolic bodies. Isak Dinesen said that if she traced her entire life, it would be the image of a stork, always carrying new life even when old, her face bird-sharp, eyes full and alive, her mouth wearing a look of glee, a smug secret knowledge as if the murky world offered a daylight message that only she and her bird and wizard and warlock friends could read. The novelist Wallace Stegner, upon meeting her, saw this quality in her immediately.

Dinesen knew others saw this. She said, "Someone looking at me would see the picture of a stork, and in that image they would feel the presence of a *Mother*, if we give and become a gift to the world. *Sibyll* if we worry overly. *Recluse* (a master of solitude) if we feel our greatest work is yet to be." She saw the figure of a regal nature in these three forms.

For Others to Play the Queen, *Be* Your Age

To learn the way in which we are above or outside of Time's grasp is to learn to travel through Time. Maturity is many ages all at once. To have the power of years requires knowing one's age. Not just knowing the year, but to be one's age. This is not the nonsensical advice to "act your age." To be powerful at fifty one must know what fifty is: what it feels like, what permissions it grants in terms of insight, confidence, different forms of compromise—and what being fifty eliminates, such as specific desires for oneself, which is replaced with a general wish to contribute. To know and respect the Enemy Time is to understand its effect upon you.

What must one do to gain eternal life? a character in a Dostoyevsky novel asks. Above all, he is told, do not lie to yourself. Stop your age machismo: stop insisting that fifty is the new forty. Do not deceive yourself. Know your age in your body and soul so that when fifty-one rolls around, you realize that it is distinct from fifty or forty-nine or twenty. Respect what the years bring and what they take so that you may know the value of being fifty. Do not hide from age so that you may know your power. You may think you want to look thirty, but who wants to *be* thirty again?

A child tracks with almost scientific discernment the differences between seven versus seven and a half or seven and three-quarters. Each month or year thus represents a triumph to the child. Know your age intimately rather than hide from it and so gain a mastery over Time.

The ultra-feminine Colette said at age sixty-five, "I

am younger now than I ever was." She noted the wealth of time and its gifts in her body. At age sixty-eight, she stopped the car on her way home from her third wedding and listened to the snow fall on a winter day in the country. Her senses were alive not just to her feelings *but to how she lived in Time*. Living richly in Time made her a very adroit time traveler. She could be old and wise and young and unpredictable. She understood her cumulative power.

When you feel a kinship with Time, you love fate and submit to it: its losses never feel like loss again but rather the restoration of timeless femininity—the second body. You are no longer just Mary or Susan or Sarah. You are a true woman.

Age may be the first time one becomes Woman herself.

Let Your Past Drop Away from You Because It's Ripe

Our Godmother Madame de Maintenon submitted to loss by abandoning her youthful illusions. In dreary middle age, one is caught between one's past and one's future. But maturity is a freedom from one's own past. "Try not to regret the past too much," Colette recalled as her method of gaining buoyancy by dumping ballast. "There is a ripeness to events, a ripeness to places, a ripeness to relations. All of them disconnect...like a child ready to be born. The child...bruises us too, yet it *must* fall.

"I love my present. I'm not ashamed of what I've had, and I'm not sad because I have it no longer."

Dwell upon the past and Time has overtaken you. "We don't make mistakes—we live!" The artist Louise Nevelson was pleased that whole memories were gobbled up by Time. Unburdened of her past, she gained a clear and uncluttered mind, free of "splinters," as she called memories. She compared forgetting to cleaning her mind with silver polish and rags "to keep it shiny"—a cleansing she found essential for creation, as it provided her with a rich inventory of half-remembered emotions and experiences.

The Russian empress Catherine the Great did not hold grudges—a case of letting the past drop like ripened fruit. She "pocketed every insult" but did not act upon old grievances. When her lover abandoned her for a lady-in-waiting, she knew he would come to realize that marital pleasures are not as good as the pleasures of respect at court that came with being the empress's favorite. At sixty, Catherine knew her lover would return to her. She held the imagination and innocence of a girl, yet she understood that "love and its illusions were stronger than the strongest diplomat."

Like a cat, let the physical body live in the moment. "Content yourself with a passing temptation, and satisfy it. What more can one be sure of than that which one holds in one's arms, at the moment one holds it in one's arms? We have so few chances to be proprietary."

When one's own past drops away, one may appreciate more keenly the great effect of women upon history. As you become more "we" than "I," your second self will become stronger. Your mysterious presence will add to the power of your physical being.

To reveal and cover ourselves in the art of presence, let us school ourselves in the mysteries as Leonardo depicted them and as the remaining Tactics will reveal. They are an expression of love beyond romance; enacting a vision of a golden world; wielding destructive power; and revealing the jewel-tone patina of the aristocracy of age.

This is how we begin to show forth the masterpiece of our lives out of the forms and colors we are given.

TACTIC 3

Become a great man who is
all woman, because the sexes do not age.
They mature into femininity.

Once upon a youthful time, men were from Mars and women from Venus. But with age, women and men arrive at the same place: maturity. Differences diminish. Men develop breasts and women's torsos thicken. Men weaken and women gain strength. Men become emotional; women turn steely. Men have midlife crises; women have midlife rebirths. Men blubber at things over which women choke back laughter. Women become as potent as teenage boys; men as mild as virgin brides.

This changes the field of sexual relations—hence power—entirely. Not only because women are now aligned with creatures less different from them, but also because they have the full expression of new capabilities.

When people are more alike than different, there is more liking and fewer differences.

Elizabeth I said she ruled as a female, but "with the heart and stomach of a king." Three hundred years later, Gustave Flaubert referred to his "cher maître" or dear master, George Sand, feminist, writer, lover of men until her death at age seventy-one: "She was a great man who was all woman." He often calls her "him." Two hundred years beyond that, Susan Sontag declared that her ambition in age was to become a great man.

In some societies, older women are privy to men's cult secrets that are rigidly kept from young women. Age allows women to use these secrets publicly. Femininity in its greatest expression includes everything: female and male, creation and destruction, laughter and seriousness.

The literal truth of this is under the skin of the painting. When we look into the Mona Lisa's eyes, we see into the artist's: she is painted directly over Leonardo's self-portrait, his fifty-year-old face. Why did he render his mature self beneath the face of a strikingly ageless woman perfectly, so that feminine features override his masculine characteristics? Part of what mesmerizes in the Mona Lisa's visage is the duality of the genders. "The painter always paints himself," Picasso said, citing Leonardo. Leonardo, who never surrendered the work, which he finished around 1503, to its presumed sitter, Lisa Gherardini, who may have commissioned it. That it was more than a portrait of a client may be why he carried it everywhere he traveled.

The Mona Lisa is a great man who is all woman, and a great woman who is a matured man.

The privilege a woman has is to regenerate herself at the expense of the weaker male. In age, woman's superiority is welcome. She may finally give up the lost quest to achieve equality with men and instead recognize her superiority—or the fact that women grow into their alpha male nature without losing their feminine ways. Men may then wonder how they may become a great man who is all woman. Faust, a scholar who sold his soul to the devil and then wanted it back, restored his lost powers by dwelling for a time in the Kingdom of the Mothers. Mature feminine perception healed and recovered his lost powers. The Greek god Dionysus wanted people to know that he had been raised as a girl. Christ's earliest and strongest supporters were women. Men school themselves in feminine mastery and leadership even today.

Time increasingly makes "male" the weaker sex, the sex vulnerable to war and decay, while the feminine unfolds as wild, justice-driven, and dominant, not self-involved. There is a yearning for the Kingdom of the Mothers today in a new, less distant breed of politician: tolerant, pluralistic, feminine, maternal, and knowing or secure, less in need of status or recognition than princes are wont to be. Throughout paternalistic Latin America, female politicians are being elected to high office. The years 2005–2006 saw the election of a woman to the presidency of Liberia, to the prime ministerial rank of Germany, to the election of the first female Speaker of the House, to the possible presidential candidacy of Hillary Clinton, fifty-seven, from whom voters polled expect greater ethics and inclusiveness than they get from male politicians.

Men and women are seeking to show these ultra-feminine qualities—voices of moral outrage and intimate empathy. Ségolène Royal, Socialist candidate for the presidency of France, calls herself an "anti-elephant" working outside of a political or institutional machine in a time when institutions have low rates of trustworthiness. A woman who runs for president of the United States would do well to cast herself as markedly female rather than as a figure who considers herself beyond any gender definition.

The mature feminine is considered more authentic and desirable. When Mario Batali branded his unique style of cooking, he ignored the Godfathers of French cuisine like the *Larousse Gastronomique*, and adopted instead the techniques and recipes of his Italian grandmother.

Qualities of Timeless Leadership Are Double-Gendered

A great man who is all woman struggles not so much against others or against herself but rather against her culture or her time. Such a person seeks to become anachronistic: she seeks ways to step outside of time rather than to become trendy.

A great man who is all woman changes her style from that of girlishly feminine youth. Mature women don't so much talk louder as more clearly. Their projects and goals become less fuzzy and erudite, more precise and down-to-earth. And so do their appetites.

A great man who is all woman becomes natural in every way. She does not force or stylize power. She relaxes her defenses. Her work matches the organic quality of her life. "Submission," once a word that had to do with sex, now characterizes a mature woman's relationship to Time, to her destiny, and to her native powers.

A great man who is all woman becomes more feminine, not less. She flirts widely with people and with possibilities. She acts with an abandon she never knew in youth. She acquires a family of alliances—a court—not just blood kin.

A great man who is all woman enacts this new advantage as a storyteller. Nothing controls Time as much as telling a story about one's life and events. A storyteller may slow down her perception of Time or speed it up. She re-creates herself as a complete being first by adjusting her language with a single word.

Rudiments of a Campaign of Orchestrated Seduction

Those who are attracted to mature feminine leadership wish to be changed, deepened, and transformed. By these means we may draw others close:

1. Use the narrative of invitation.

Men lead by *imitation*, inspiring like behavior in others. Young women lead by *inspiration* and allure. But mature women lead by *invitation*: the promise of an open, experimental, joyous experience.

> In age, one does not so much seduce a boy
>
> (or men, or women, or crowds)
>
> as help him take her.

In a world where the young are asked to make choices about everything from cereal to partners, a new vocabulary is needed. Because choice suggests the outcome of an argument. That is how an argument is settled: choosing one alternative over another; one worldview at the expense of another that also has interesting features.

A different Narrative is *invitation*; the mechanism is acceptance and a forfeit of will.

Its environment is surprise, "wonder," and a discovery that is not simple but full of powerful shared energy. Invitations are very much like looking at a great painting: an image like the Mona Lisa is an invitation.

Keep this script in mind. Allow it to be the background music to your encounters: "Who else can give you what you get from me?" one's invitation might say. "Who sidesteps resentments, cliques, and cul-de-sacs of hierarchy better than I do? And then, once others arrive and you become the center, remind yourself, I'm here as if from another field, another place, another world. Let's talk. Maybe you'll become part of my circle, my network."

The years of loss show a woman how she has everything she needs. Even in conflict, she need not choose or take sides. Inaction is preferable. You may refer to the need for a decision countless times. Elizabeth I was fond of this technique. She was already in a leadership position, so choice would have set up antagonisms. *Making no choice keeps the invitation widely open.* This is as simple, often, as replacing the word "or" with "and" and the word "should" with "could." By such shifts in how one tells a story, one relies upon the language of open invitation.

The Queen knows her power comes not from the mastery of the master, but the mystery of the "mistress" who can play the hostess and friend.

2. Welcome a new sense of reality breaking through, including anger.

This is a tone change in mature stories: mature women no longer wish to have to fight their way into the old-boys' club. They are tired of aspiring to join or even appearing to want to join the old elephants. They want to be non-elephants. Or even more, anti-elephants. They want to create realms that are different from the prevailing forces of power. When Ségolène Royal, fifty-two, campaigned for the presidency of France, she stood in opposition to the male campaigners, on a completely different platform, against airy ideas and for such "trivial" matters as schools, child rearing, and the effects of popular culture. In effect, she ran against France's political culture—male-dominated and entrenched—and the culture struck back, ridiculing her as a soap bubble borne aloft by a momentary gust of public infatuation. She was a soap bubble in terms of a magic shimmer, for she won her party's nomination.

Electorates, consumers, followers want women to voice the outrage they feel, not at a bitchy level but at a higher moral plane. They want their anger voiced in public, but anger as a woman can articulate it with a sense of moral correction. Voters want to hear a woman sound off with a Mosaic dignity—conviction stated with calm control and unrelenting purpose.

A strong leader like Hillary Clinton would be damned

not if she were outspoken, but only if she were not angry enough. Women acquire depth and complexity with age that encourages them to take on the deeply wrinkled, slow-moving elephants. Some cultures burn such women, some hide them in nunneries, some turn away their attention. Others elect them queens and finally come to applaud their visions.

3. Recognize that survival isn't everything; love is.

This is the supreme invitation, the most telling element of the new narrative of maturity. In youth, "survival" was the word most often repeated. Now love is the more critical need: one needs to have love and to give it. And not just any love but unconditional love—love for all that you are, not for a few select parts of you. Elizabeth I sought her subjects' unconditional love. Love must be the reason an electorate votes for a woman candidate, because rationality won't win her an election. Unconditional love eliminates the threat stirred by sexuality.

"Amor mundi" is the philosopher Hannah Arendt's phrase for her notion of unconditional love of the world. It was an odd notion for a woman who at age fifty-two had seen the political monstrosities of war and genocide up close.

Eleanor of Aquitaine developed a new story of power: it was a court of love. Eleanor Roosevelt developed a new story of politics: acts of sacrifice and love. The women running for high office in countries throughout the world are telling a story that runs counter to remoteness and abstraction, ideological retrenchment, and male domination itself. The world is wide open for women's invitations to a new way of practical and spiritual vision. As the political classes and the power elite become increasingly alien to people, as institutions—the church, the military, the large corporations—become less trustworthy, it falls to a woman to remake the very nature of institutional life.

4. In telling the new story, stop producing or changing or bettering yourself. Harvest all that you have.

A young woman may work as she breathes, very fast, automatically. She may swallow the world around her and it will come out in words, paintings, decisions, babies. Later in life she may complain of being unable to work, of finding focus torture. She may feel neither fish nor fowl. That is when everything changes: focus, intent, habit. She no longer produces; she harvests. One may be shameless about harvesting the effects of age. Elizabeth I would, at times, bare her royal bosom, literally show her aging breasts at court, which gave wags much fuel for satire. The rare moments of brazen self-exposure sent a message: that she was beyond shame, and wild, needing to make no explanations. It was an invitation for the court to see that she was a woman and a monarch who could be as she pleased.

5. Relax your effort from doing to being and thereby adopt a deliberately unproductive productiveness.

To draw others into one's power or story is to no longer care if one's activity results in something splendid or even finished. One does what one most desires, and if the work is flawed or unfinished, or if it appeals only to oneself, so be it. *More exciting than mastery is a work that may be fully "unmastered."* Raw. Begun and abandoned, but full of a new energy unlike the focused energy of youth. Ripeness is a condition of roundness but it is also furrowed and even ravaged. It bears the marks of age.

The face of feminine command
directs attention away from oneself and
increasingly to others and to the world at large.
Therein is found true sleeping beauty.

Picasso saw in Gertrude Stein a force that Renaissance artists discerned in women whom they transformed into paintings of immortal beauties. When
Stein first looked at the portrait of herself that Picasso
painted, she cried, "That doesn't look like me at all."
He replied, "It will." He was right. Stein attained a look
entirely imperial, commanding, and more irresistibly
attractive with Time. She grew into her destiny as the
timeless sage whose spirit Picasso recognized in her.

A woman's identity and power may be read largely
in her face, which comes to seem to her like a stranger's
in age. That is because the face is more naked in maturity than ever before. As it loses its soft girlish features

it attains a brave beauty that attracts others and perhaps intimidates them. To express one's full power, one is to appreciate how brave beauty is expressed and perceived, and how we—artists of a masterpiece of maturity—may influence the ways in which we are seen. For women do not grow invisible with Time. They grow ever more noticeable. To attain a commanding presence requires that one express the elements of maturity boldly and deliberately.

What, then, is the face of feminine command?

There are four such faces. Each is the external portrait of an internal script of leadership and self-esteem. Each face offers a different approach to the daunting fears of age: becoming invisible and being underestimated. Each self-portrait affords a way of staying visible and adored.

A painter looks beyond the surface to a deeper and more lasting quality of beauty. Yes, a woman loses her usefulness to others as she leaves the career heights and as her family disperses. Her qualities then become intangible, expressed as warmth or wisdom. She becomes like a picture or a statue to covet. People may enjoy the statue and the picture but not know what to do with them. So mentally they store her in some out-of-the-way temple unprofaned by cold analysis. After the first blush of beauty fades, *people love a woman without merely loving themselves.* That is the whole secret of how we come to represent the beautiful, the good and the "one truth" of love, friendship, art, devotion, and faith. That is the face of feminine command. It reflects these timeless qualities, not personality. Feminine command has none of the features of youth...it has none of the features of "personality." It is defined as iconic.

> When you feel your own "self" getting less intense, you love people and things for what they are in themselves, what they represent in the eyes of your soul, and not at all for what they will contribute to your own destiny.

Maturity reflects *only love and beauty, not necessarily others' needs*...One becomes the expression of feminine energy:

In any previous age, sex was strength. Neither art nor beauty was needed. Every one, even among Puritans, knew that neither Diana of the Ephesians nor any of the Oriental goddesses was worshipped for her beauty. She was [a] goddess because of her force; she was the animated dynamo . . . the greatest and most mysterious of all energies.

—HENRY ADAMS

How you are seen is more important than how you look. You have control over how you appear to others. If you look at yourself in an iconic mirror, like that of Leonardo's painting, your beauty softens. You do not see the pores and lines; you see your mystery and the fullness of femininity reflected back to you. And that is what you project to others.

Beautiful as Coretta Scott King was in youth, she became mesmerizing only in the years after her husband's death, when the fleetingness of life and love changed the way the public saw her face. Tragedy and loss could have destroyed her beauty. But she became more than attractive; she became iconic. Iconic beauty gives one access, leeway, and attention of a kind unknown in youth. An observer may be compelled to look more closely at a face with the mystery of life etched upon it. Reduced to her essence by her terrible loss, King became a figure of brave beauty as she aged. The beauty into which one grows captures the sting of the fleetingness of the world.

A woman, like an artist, has the *power to make a person see as she wishes him to see.*

Since human life is fleeting, like flowers, beautiful

women embody not only elegance but also the reality and slight sorrow of life in time. The deep humanity rises to the surface. They convey elements of the dark, profound, and tranquil color of the universe.

> *At the age of fifty women begin a new kind of beauty, as one might take up a new career late in life, or as ground that is no longer any good for vines can be used for growing beet. Around these features a new youthfulness starts to flourish.*
>
> —MARCEL PROUST

So Isak Dinesen at thirty appeared modest and unremarkable. But at sixty she was commanding, riveting, her face a riverbed of wrinkles, her eyes black shiny coals. At age sixty-one Eleanor Roosevelt was more mesmerizing than in her youth. She knew that new porcelain caps had helped, but also that in age one is responsible for one's face. Hers bore her choice to love people no matter what they did and to help others and rescue them. Her beauty became one with her work...it identified her; her face communicated her commitment to vast and selfless causes. Icons of Eleanor—photos of her—were kept on display for years in homes all over the world. Her face gave people pleasure; it was the picture of beauty beyond beauty. We barely have a language in which to chart the nature of this new-older beauty. It expresses openness, humor, and the "we" before the "I."

Four Faces of Female Command

Let the image of a flower teach us a new language for capturing beauty beyond beauty. Throughout Colette's existence, she said, "I have studied the flowering more than any other stage of life. It is there, for me, that the essential drama resides."

Flowering is a summit. As youth is a bud, maturity is a flower.

Four flowers represent increasingly commanding levels of brave beauty. Each is an iconic look by which one may be seen, heard, and respected.

Four styles define the presence of brave beauty to tell a new story of age. The face of youth is despotically familiar. It exerts an aesthetic hold upon observers. Few know how to read the face of beauty beyond beauty. Yet distinctions are power: a medical student learns ten thousand new words: knowing the difference between duodenum and jejunum helps to make a person a doctor. To define the four faces of command is to see them worn proudly by their possessor and to etch them into our minds as a new facial heraldry. The qualities we hold in our mind eventually show up on our face. It is not just a matter of saying one grows into a brave beauty in age. It is using a new visual vocabulary as we judge ourselves on our appearance.

There is another element to this analysis of feminine command. The more we relax into the beauty of age, the happier we are. Each of the four faces represents a new level of alliance with Time.

ONES: *She Who Is Adored*

Symbol: *A beautiful flower*
Tactic: Like one beautiful flower, Ones makes the surrounding elements more glorious by their presence.
Source of power: Evoking astonishment

Ones seem ageless. They ground their presence in the discipline with which they maintain their youth. But this keeps them dependent on the kindness of Time to maintain their appearance. This is not the best bet to make, because Time can be very fickle.

A person whose appearance or actions people remark upon is typically a One: Catherine Deneuve, Kim Basinger, Julia Roberts. A performance of surpassing loveliness is often the work of a One. They draw attention to themselves.

There is nothing selfish or unusually narcissistic about Ones. They wish to spread their glory. A well-known news anchor, for example, smiles at a person she is interviewing: the object of her regard seems more striking by virtue of her attention. Brilliant *Vogue* editor Anna Wintour's conferring praise upon a designer makes both the designer and Wintour herself more striking.

Communicating in this way means always being aware of oneself as a focal point. As she aged Louise Nevelson looked like a beautiful clown, with her Vaselined face and furry dark fake-lashed eyes: she wasn't the least secretive about her age. She wore age as a badge of honor. Age became an act to amuse herself and others. "When I'm the star, I never get bored," said Nevelson, the boldest and most original American sculptor of the twentieth century. When she was in her sixties, her presence became more powerful than ever. She dramatized her appearance more than when she was young. She wore opulent black materials, considering herself "the empress of art." "No woman should enter a room without making as extraordinary a first impression as possible." She never complained of feeling overdressed, only underdressed. Her clothes were loose and her shoes were flat so she could take great strides. "I'm what you call a real collage," she said. She washed her face in olive oil and wore two sets of false eyelashes at the same time.

Ones retain their thunder *while at the same time acquiring the mercy and power of age*. Blustery they might be; their tough persona covers a soft interior. Think of Meryl Streep's star turn as the editor in chief of

Runway, the magazine in *The Devil Wears Prada*. The editor Streep portrays is demanding and insistent, but as a way of mirroring in others her own behavior to inspire a high level of creativity. Streep's character is so over the top she is almost comical. Ones stay just this side of the divide between being serious and being hyperdramatic.

Ones epitomize the allure of the single flower. They want to be singular in the degree to which they are noticed.

Their physical beauty draws others to mirror themselves in their presence. In Shakespeare's play *Antony and Cleopatra*, the Roman warrior Antony leaves his family and home to live with the Egyptian queen Cleopatra. He is lured by her One energy and full-scale charm to mirror himself in Cleopatra's eyes: her beauty, often portrayed as female handsomeness and not youthful prettiness, makes him feel strong and powerful. The mirror is Cleopatra's power. Her power regenerates him. It is transferable. The pleasures Antony derives from Cleopatra are not inebriating but life-affirming. ("The nobleness of life is to do this.") Cleopatra has a refined sense of power: she knows that it must be both masculine and feminine. The power Cleopatra affords Antony is that of choosing the court versus empire, mature womanliness versus rational masculinity. Empire is policing and necessary, but feasting and loving are not to be regretted but to be sought after. That is her invitation.

One's power is brave. It is also highly experimental. It speaks of a great faith in the self. "To be praised, one must praise oneself," the female Machiavel Diane de Poitiers said. Diane, twenty years older than the French king Henri II, mesmerized him. She became his mistress when she was thirty-five and he was the fifteen-year-old prince. Upon his coronation, she became co-regent in charge of his foreign policy and his money, and made the French court a lively and intellectual center. But their very strength is also their weakness: Ones are dependent on others to mirror or admire their beauty. Anaïs Nin was a modern Cleopatra and Diane combined: sixty-three years old before the diary that she had been writing for three decades—and rejected for almost that long—was finally published. Late success burnished Nin's captivating presence. She wore flowing dresses, her face a powdered mask, her voice a whisper: her femininity the basis for a free and adventurous life made up of famous friends, beautiful clothes, love affairs, and the uncompromising work of an artist. Men were so transfixed that Nin entered into two marriages with two different men on two separate coasts at the same time: "I live out my dreams." She seemed caught in amber, carrying on with youthful energy. Each husband, like Antony, derived power from Nin's presence.

The strategy of Ones, then, is to attract others to mirror their presence. It is a very tight hold, and Ones' arena is therefore centered upon their physical presence and their stories of strength and heroism. The power of mature presence offers a wider arena, as we shall see.

Singularity defines Ones' lives. They favor hermetically sealed environments: others are invited inside their habitats only and for so long as the guests mirror back Ones' beauty and do not add much of themselves. Antony begs, "I am dying, Egypt, dying," and Cleopatra interrupts him with a speech about *her* needs. Access to Ones is rare and privileged and those who are invited into their proximity are not permitted to add much of themselves.

Ones' energy is defined and limited by their presence. *A single flower is never as commanding as a field.* Ones define themselves as being in constant pursuit of youthfulness. Ones' beauty, like a single flower, eventually fades.

A One may use her face as a stand-in for herself and as an object of her own amusement. The persona is an assertive mask impossible to ignore, and difficult to change. As she aged, Nevelson believed that without her regalia, dress, makeup, and reputation, she would be unnoticed and unloved. "It isn't just the work, but what you put in the work, and who you are, and how you present things . . . it all adds up." Insecurity over her appearance drove Nevelson to extremes.

Charm is a limiting quality. A One develops into a Two when she recognizes that a more commanding presence *captures the eye and evades it at the same time.*

A principle of visual energy, known to Leonardo, is that beauty is determined less by elements in its focus than by qualities at the periphery. In a room, for example, a sofa or any piece of furniture in the center is noticed first, while cherished mementos—photos, souvenirs, books—relegated to the walls and corners seem to go unnoticed. Yet the presence of items at the periphery changes the ambience or energy of the entire room. Leonardo deliberately painted the Mona Lisa so that the viewer's eye does not dwell upon the center of her face. The dark sfumato and the layers of earth-toned paints Leonardo patiently added one upon the other are meant to keep the eye moving across her face, and as it moves, her expression changes from smiling to serious . . . and so she seems to be alive.

To shift the viewer's eye off center to the gathering and expanding mystery of a woman's presence, a One must call upon more mature qualities of interaction, as epitomized by the next level of power.

TWOS: She Who Educates

Symbol: *A flower without color*
Tactic: The rule of paradox
Source of power: Cool eros

A flower without color is beautiful to senses beyond the eye and nose. A flower without color evokes a presence of a mystery difficult to pinpoint but worth understanding. It is a flower whose appeal comes from its abstract form or place in one's memory or imagination. It draws on the idea of flowers and of fragrances.

A flower without color has the beauty of pure whiteness. Art and nature unite virginally in this austere style. As in pure snow, it is the silver that entrances, not the mounds of ice.

Like that flower, a Two woman conjures a presence that does not entirely depend upon her physical appearance. She has an exquisite modesty that defers to a place, a time (like sunset), or a conversation with others. She begins her move off center: she both appears and disappears, and this is a hallmark of Twos' brave beauty.

Two energy is a characteristic one finds also in the façades of the most interesting buildings. The architect of the rebuilt Museum of Modern Art in New York City told the board of directors, "Raise enough money and I'll make you a beautiful building. Raise even more and I'll make the building disappear." The deferential building he created allows visitors to be drawn to it yet be undistracted by the architecture and able to focus on the art inside. A woman like a building has more presence by the *suggestion* of her presence, by the teasing of attention more than by a mirrorlike hold upon it. Evading the eye is a practice Twos cultivate. The more a woman defers attention from herself yet remains alluring by other means, the more energy and power she commands.

A Two woman does this by taking on the qualities of a teacher who *teaches who she is*.

Twos are beautiful but not in a way that inspires comments, as do Ones. *They do not seduce clients by charm or flirtation; they educate others in the elements that make them unique.* The designer Vera Wang, whose face is almost ageless, is the emblem of simplicity, her face displaying qualities of femininity and masculinity both. Wang has taught a generation of brides how to dress; she has taught the bridal industry a new level of ritual and elegance in celebrations. She does not sell herself. Her perspective is wider. She does not seduce or charm. She teaches others her point of view, her interest—not in time-bound trends (like Ones) but in the timeless things: ritual events, like weddings as mythic experiences. Wang has become the symbol of something larger than herself. The journalist Christiane Amanpour is a Two in whom one sees foremost the face of courage, dedication, and calm. She reports the news but she also teaches who she is: fearless, sharp, as if born to the task she has taken on.

Charmers (Ones) are cultural barometers. But the

Teacher—as Twos often are—has the more mature relationship to Time. She changes people by evoking the cyclical tradition, the deeper news, the ritualistic experience. By such means she awakens them to the new and reassures them with the old or timeless. These are what she talks about and instructs in. She begins to peel herself away from the clock, from the new, but not entirely. She is still identified with a flower, with the passing illusions and beauties; though a mystical "colorless" flower.

She is quieter than Ones. The actress Judi Dench barely moves onstage, her trademark quality is a centered stillness that compels viewers' attention upon her, no matter what else is going on elsewhere onstage. This stillness is like the silver in ice.

Twos bloom after a dramatic departure or conversion from youthful ways. They are created almost out of a repudiation of youth—as if a strong turning away from youth made commitment to maturity stronger. The poet Elizabeth Barrett Browning was as a young woman confined to her bed: sick and weak or perhaps in equal measures fearful and repressed by a tyrannical father. Suddenly, the poet Robert Browning arrived at her bedside to pay her literary homage, and his love transformed her. She rose from her sickbed in a burst of energy, married him, made a hearty voyage with him to Italy, where they worked, had a son, and loved each other for years. She did not try to relive her youth.

She abandoned it and welcomed the fact that later in life, in her mature years, she made up for the trepidations of her youth.

Perhaps because of this conversion, Two energy is greater than One energy. Twos find energy in breaking the hold on their youth. When a person wants out of the cocoon of a typical or habitual job to run for office or to ascend into some institutional stratosphere like heading an orchestra or becoming elevated to company president, then she does well to turn herself into a Teacher, stamped by her mission and by modes of expression that are both mothering and loving.

A Two may be dangerously seductive because of her advancing age. A double chin makes Willa Cather's Myra Henshaw hold her head high, and Colette's Lea fastens a choker of pearls around her thickening neck. Twos give the impression of being old and young—erotic forces with an ethereal or otherworldly presence. The decorator Elsie de Wolfe, at ninety-one, was beautiful: slim as a girl, in a dress of white muslin, with a choker of sapphires at her throat. Twin strands of motherliness and youthfulness make it hard to literalize a Two's age. A Two prominent in Texas society decided at age sixty to wear skirts again because she had great legs. Eyes followed her everywhere, and when she turned around and people saw her God-given face, they were shocked—at which point she lit up in a big showy smile.

Twos are figures of ambiguity, irony, and ambivalence, doubleness, contradiction, paradox, *"a simultaneous dependence-independence"* with people in whose lives they find themselves. They adopt these forms of style and communication; doing so gives them more leeway than clinging to youthful beauty. It not only gives them confidence, it attracts others to this confidence. Twos gain energy and attractiveness when they display ambivalence, that is, keep two points of view alive at the same time. Elizabeth I was a Two at her most political. Her ambivalence about marrying kept her court guessing. Jackie Onassis was "caught in the gap between ingénue and empress, between innocence and worldliness." As she matured, she became a Two. She renounced the ruby red Chanels of her youth for soft gray and black cashmeres—a disappearing, eye-evading MOMA, yet the center of attention everywhere.

While others do not usually remark upon the cool and spectral quality of Twos' beauty, they certainly are aroused by it, because it is such a unique combination of real and fantasy image. Two energy is stereoscopic—doubled—making Twos seem larger and stronger in iconic presence. Martha Stewart is more like Shakespeare's most mature character, Rosalind, who teaches young Orlando how to love her. Martha is a teacher of style as a kind of cool love. The character she is often considered, the ambitious and vengeful Lady Macbeth, is wrong. Her energy is mouthy, pushy, opinionated—wonderful and difficult. Twos do not care if they are charming: rather, their prickliness is their kind of charm. Teachers, perfectionists, they believe adoration or admiration to be overrated as goals.

Condoleezza Rice and Hillary Clinton have great Two energy: they are clear symbols of purpose—the flower without color. A mission, like a colorless flower, is larger than its representative.

Twos have better command than Ones of the paradox of desire and detachment. They find a middle ground in devotion. They do not seek others' imitation of them, as Ones do. Twos cast a wide circle of influence, however: they create philosophies or points of view in which others find their own identity. Twos welcome a wider range of people different from themselves. Thus Twos build formidable institutions. Their attractiveness to others increases as they begin to evade the eye.

Diana Vreeland, the legendary editor of *Vogue* in the 1960s, was called ugly by her own mother. She began as a One (in which people comment on your looks for good *or* bad) and developed into a Two. She became visible for her opinions—funny and ironic—on others' looks and so evaded the eye. She issued pronouncements on fashion that led her industry and the culture. A true Two, she taught an *idea* of beauty, bold and brave, and yet was compellingly detached from it: a colorless flower. An idea of beauty is not just a trend.

By such means, Twos age better than Ones. At age seventy-four in 1961, the painter Georgia O'Keeffe, her face marked by lines and wrinkles, made for an even more mesmerizing portrait than the camera had captured of her forty years earlier. Her face showed an intimate knowledge of solitude and endurance and was deliberate and beautiful.

O'Keeffe was a great artist whose presence very much suggested the teacher who stands behind her mission, not in front of it. She was opinionated about other people's lives—as a mentor to artists and a benefactor to the people of her desert community. Her senses were completely alert and tuned to the splendors around her, which made her strong personality seem larger, as if one with the strong and gorgeous landscape. "Georgia feels and sees the space and what it does to you, and allows you to feel and see it too." By the time she was seventy-eight, her iron-rod posture and regal bearing gave the impression of great strength and stature. Her jawline remained as hard as the Abiquiu cliffs in which she made her matriarchal home, two hours outside of Albuquerque. At elegant gatherings, like her art opening, she stood out among the women in jewels and gowns wearing her tailored black suit with a spot of silver glistening at her throat.

Twos do not conform to style; they need only an accoutrement to be noticed.

Twos are especially likely to give way to the "great man" in themselves. As O'Keeffe approached the age of sixty-nine, people remarked often on her many strong "masculine" qualities: her driving ambition, immense self-confidence (she believed that if she wanted something badly enough, she would be able to get it), uncompromising will, intimidating presence, and absorption in her work. It was said of her, "She has a shotgun—and she uses it." Whether or not this was so, she gave the impression that her art, and by extension, she herself, had absolute rights, and she seemed oddly unaware of the havoc this self-centered attitude could cause in others.

Twos create matriarchal spaces of a dreamy awe, but they become fierce leaders locked in the center and possessed by the center. This is their limitation. Ones depend on organizational platforms not created by them but that they nevertheless mirror. Twos prefer having one foot in the worlds of their own creation. They don't merely enhance a television news division or a magazine conglomerate, they create institutions in their own image. Jackie Kennedy redefined her husband's presidency as Camelot, and she became its imperial Guinevere. O'Keeffe built a home in the desert, but what made the place soulful beyond any physical trapping was how she captured and extended this desert landscape in her paintings. Martha Stewart's Omnimedia is a company with so many alliances that it is difficult to chart the boundaries, except the boundaries of her own interests.

To become a teacher, to value ambivalence, to define a style with committed but ultimately deferential modesty—by these means Twos tend to be larger in commanding presence than Ones. Twos tend to be professional loners, valuing privacy yet also at the center of vast circles and professional families who think they know the pivotal Twos.

Twos resist Time's impact better than Ones, but not as well or for as long as they might.

THREES: *She Who Steadies*

Symbol: *The profound flower*
Tactic: Female stoicism
Source of power: Artful artlessness

Imagine that snow has covered hundreds of mountains but one. The exceptional, unique, and aberrant is the domain of Threes. Where Threes show up, the other world—the mystery of creation and destruction, of nature, of the eternal cycle of birth and death—has begun to invade the world of ordinary senses. The *profound flower* is the icon of maturity that has become highly symbolic. What is a "profound flower" but a feeling, a symbolic form that may not be taught—as is Twos' mien—but evoked?

Threes do not merely educate. Threes change the nature of their own reality: they charm, they educate, as do Ones and Twos, but in ways entirely their own, by enveloping others in worlds of their own expression. Twos create visions of a golden world, something beyond literal reality. A Two, for example, would teach others about the efforts of governments to address conflict. That is a kind of mission. But a Three like Emily Dickinson, the poet and recluse of Amherst, opened her soul to others, and by so doing, taught them about *her* world, her vision of hope, despair, and a higher reality. Dickinson was highly reclusive yet a powerful presence to those with whom she made her rare contacts. In her lifetime she made herself known to those she felt would understand the depths of her being. To be in contact with Dickinson—the person and her writing—was to feel the mystery of the universe and the woman herself. She would always be part of a world others were outside of, but might aspire to reach. That aspect of otherworldliness made her friendships strong, linked to her at a level of expression deep and honest and devoted: which elicited others' depths and devotion. Even strangers who corresponded with Emily Dickinson felt a shared, strong intimacy with her based upon her insights about life, not revelations about her life. Threes have a strong but diffuse sense of their personalities. They are not confessional; rather they want to be known and understood, not merely seen or recognized. In this desire, they regard unconditional love as a fact, not a wish. Others who come into their presence feel acceptance, not their judgment.

There is an important difference between Twos and Threes. A Two like O'Keeffe was a loner and ornery in her judgments. A Three draws upon the practice of female stoicism: a philosophy that maintains that external events should not influence a person's character or responses. In good or bad times, Threes remain the same, and essentially optimistic. Even in the worst straits, a Three considers herself free and happy. She practices resistance by optimism: a belief deep down that the world is a comedy. This is the source of Threes' grace. All Threes have some degree of laughter at the ready. Dickinson wrote with comic wit and irony. Threes cultivate a clownishness in their character and trust that others will appreciate it. One single bare mountain among the majestic snowy peaks is ethereal but also comical. Charmers (Ones) take themselves seriously. Teachers (Twos) are serious about their ideas, but female stoics sense that all is a divine comedy—and that the best way to be a serious and appreciative member of the mature human race is to take matters lightly.

Threes are fearless largely because of their stoical view. Nothing bad ever happens to Threes because they have no category for judging bad from good. They experiment with ideas and relationships. Nothing is dismissed as ridiculous.

Ones show intense feelings of pain and pleasure and inspire people to mirror their reactions. Twos filter their reactions: joy is mixed with sorrow, ambivalence, or push and pull. Threes, however, barely react, whatever the circumstances. You always know what Ones are feeling, about Twos you may guess and will always be half right. But to be in a Three's presence is to feel a vast sense of their command of emotions.

There is a strange kind of beauty available to women who are endowed with extraordinary sensitivity; this beauty attaches not only to their work or appearance but to their being. Becoming the profound flower can evoke more than adoration (which is how others relate to Ones) or inspire aspiration (as with Twos). Surrender is the quintessential habit of Threes. Their ability to be influenced and not merely influence others allows them to create a commanding presence. Because Threes are at ease in submitting to fate, they elicit submission from others.

Colette's appearance was remembered by a young lover as "a power whose shock was sweet to me.... I surrendered to that protective influence that Colette promised me with her first glance."

Perfection is not important, and Threes do not

try to overcorrect for flaws or mask imperfections. Rather, they expect to be loved for them; and if not, too bad. Colette's young lover saw her wearing her bathing costume: it clung to a body that by modern standards would be called obese. But fat women, when they are fit, are often much sexier half-naked than dressed, and Colette was still limber and superbly muscled, with Venusian breasts and the biceps of a discus thrower.

Threes love being naked in thought or appearance, one bare mountain in snowy realms. They are brilliant at surrendering themselves to fate and to the course of nature. They are all-accepting. It is an aspect of their confidence. They do not take cover in ambivalence. The more they depart from youthful attractiveness, the more they love themselves, and this love is infectious: as was said of the writer and twentieth-century *saloniste* Gertrude Stein:

> *Gertrude Stein is a great beauty. No, not for me, not at first . . . She, though, carries herself as if she is an object of desire. She carries herself* as if she is her own object of desire [my emphasis]. *Self-induced lust is addictive in its effect. Prolonged exposure makes those around them weak and helpless.*

Stein's voice was in keeping with her appearance. Her writing is very like the one bare mountain, spare and strange, a language all her own and full of wit: a rose is a rose is a rose.

The medieval queen Eleanor of Aquitaine was majestic and comedic. She lit out from the country that she ruled as queen beside her unfaithful husband to create a new kind of society—a court of love—in her home country of Poitiers. In her government love was law. Crimes were crimes against love. By such a reversal of tradition, she made the warring tribes of Europe seriously fighting over territory and booty seem nonsensical. Comedy always makes so-called tragic reality seem hopelessly stupid. A profound flower, Eleanor was the one peak without snow in a snowy land. Her presence in Europe of the twelfth century reversed the norms of living. Her court of love was a court that attracted youth who wanted no part of property or war. These were second- and third-born children for whom inheritance was impossible. Eleanor's court became as influential as Emily Dickinson's attic retreat, as Gertrude Stein's atelier, and as Cicely Saunders's hospice, St. Christopher's: self-created realms that stood apart from the norm.

Small circles generate big changes. Threes revel in small kingdoms. They change the dominant culture by the steadfast nature of their optimism and their goal of pleasure more than mission or ideas as Teacher Twos insist upon...Stein's salon became a focal point for modern art and modernist thinking. *The source of power is pleasure, which is the most subversive strategy of all.*

Threes' sensuality is highly spiritual. They align themselves with hardship more than Ones or Twos. But they transform pain and suffering into golden worlds. And they transform loss into gain—and more: pleasure.

They don't stand for a cause the way a Two politician/teacher may stand for improved health care. Threes not only pepper their talk with ideas about change—like a hospice movement—but deepen their commitment to change by adding to their mission the language of love, God, life, hope, despair... Threes evoke a beauty that overrides despair: the mountain that is aberrant and abundant.

The mature Florence Nightingale looked like a bare mountain among the snowy peaks of bedcovers. When she retreated to her bedroom, where she spent her last decade of life, tucked into her bed from 1896 until 1910, when she died, only her head was visible and dominated the setting like an oracle whose wispy smoke rose out of a sacred tumulus. This is not to make light of the stress that forced her retreat. But photographs of Florence disappearing among the bedsheets and at the time, holding forth to visitors has a slightly comic edge. Was she spiritually aloof or sensuously present? Both. There is a very subtle irony in Threes; their style does not break down into stark opposites, as Twos do. Their presence suggests a uniqueness in which unlikely qualities exist together. The famous and the powerful came in droves to consult Florence Nightingale in that chamber to learn about eradicating disease and improving public health. From there she designed the sewer system of London, the profession of nursing, and the systemization of medical records. Had Florence Nightingale been more involved in the social world, she would have been relegated to its edges. *That she established her own center at its periphery gave her power,* like the Mona Lisa in her room at the Louvre. Beatrice spoke to Dante from Paradise, Isak Dinesen from Africa: a world apart *and* part of power.

A Two may become a Three as her life changes and losses burnish her image. Barbara Jordan, who had a magnificent career in the Senate, was a Two in her presence. When she resigned her seat at the age of forty-three she became more typical of a Three. As a senator, she was a symbol of moral energy, her rhetoric a combination of Bessie Smith and Winston Churchill. But as a retired senator, she was uncompromised, her distance from conventional power conferring a new dignity and grace upon her. The most highly esteemed lawyers in Texas who wanted to be judges made the pilgrimage to her office where she, in her fifties, interviewed them, saving the most important question for last: "If

Governor Ann Richards appoints you, what will you owe her in return?" Most candidates assumed Jordan wanted them to say that they would owe the governor loyalty, or a campaign contribution. There was only one right answer for Jordan: "I owe the governor nothing. My obligation is to the people of Texas." Her sense of humor and freedom to prick the bubble of others' seriousness was how she made people view themselves as exceptions too, the one bare and independent mountain. Humble singularity is dazzling Three energy.

A Three might be stripped of her job and her health, as in Jordan's case. The more essentialist or pared down her circumstances, the more a Three will thrive, the greater her influence and power become. Threes' losses are not disasters but rather focusing mechanisms to help them stand apart like bare and unique mountains upon a spiritual plane. A little boy once brought Jordan a Bible to sign. Asked why, she said, "He must have thought I wrote it."

But even Three magic has limits. There is one more level in the climb to the command presence of mature power.

FOURS: She Who Is Magically Everywhere

Symbol: *Where the sun shines brightly at midnight*
Tactic: Female trickster
Source of power: Submission

Fours go beyond a flower, and beyond a mountain that contains fields of flowers. Fours are the foundation for *flowering*, the returning sun, and the cool night's ease. There is a saying that when it is midnight in Japan, the sun is shining in Silla, South Korea. It is considered an exalted form of mind and persona to evoke a place that is physically remote. To see Silla when you are a world away is to have a mind and presence that operates without boundaries. People who possess Four energy are said to have the quality of being in two places at once. At a spiritual retreat, a Four might laugh upon noticing a painting that looks unconsciously sexy. At a dinner in New York a Four may conjure in her mind an anger over the hunger in South Africa, or in the full bloom of health she may feel the anguish of the sick and dying. Fours have a protean quality that shows up in photos: a Four tends to look completely different in different images—a reflection of her range of openness to the fleetingness of life, where one is not only related to a wide family of friends and fellow travelers, but more: Time and Space being illusory, one also is always alive to the variety of human states.

Four is a state of mind. Mature power ascends into the Four state from time to time. Few women sustain Four energy.

When a woman reaches the very peak of her symbolic beauty, she is sometimes described as a source of light. This is how her physical form registers on others. Fours are radiant. Martha Gellhorn, a war journalist and wife of Ernest Hemingway, the only one of his wives who stood up to his abusive behavior, said of Eleanor Roosevelt, "She gave off light. I cannot explain it better. We all know people like this, almost pathologically modest, who live for being useful and who, because of that, are very brave." Upon Eleanor's death, Gellhorn wrote, "I always knew she was something so rare that there's no name for it, *more than a saint, a saint who took on the experiences of everyday life, an absolutely unfrightened, self-less woman whose heart never went wrong* [my italics]." That selflessness seems to dissolve physical limits...

In a Four's presence, Time stops for a time. *Fours are like Tricksters in that they take a position at the cross-roads of life. They show up at turning points in people's lives* and tend to change the lives of those who come into contact with them, no matter how brief their contact. Fours have a talent for finding ways in which to matter to many people. Twos undergo a change or conversion. Fours prompt it in others.

The logic of Four's power may be stated this way: a contradiction in space-time is not a contradiction when seen from a higher (integrated) perspective. A truly commanding woman—calm and alert in her person—makes others visualize such an integrated world, a world of higher reality lying beyond our ordinary senses. At its sight we are struck with the feeling of austerity. Fours communicate an austerity: they may have wealth or fame or certainty but refrain from displaying it. Instead, a kind of majesty surrounds them. Light-filled, or spectral, or haunting: these are Four qualities.

As Ones depend on adoration, Twos upon admiration, Threes upon art, Fours upon magic, we see that the heat of emotion cools and the emotions themselves become stronger.

In this, Fours are most like works of art. The Mona Lisa inhabits the Louvre in Paris, yet to be in her presence is to feel transported to sixteenth-century Florence and to see into the mystery of timeless, undying art. One stands before a great work of art and forgets oneself, forgets even that one is breathing. For Fours, Time and Space do not exist . . . Time can always be revoked. Space is multiple.

A woman who achieves the Four level of beauty has a force almost as great as Time's. Her maturity does not depend upon her personality, individuality, beauty, or commitment to teach. Yet Four beauty includes all the striking loveliness of Ones, all the doubleness of Twos, all the elegant stoicism of Threes, and the addition of the selfless and unself-conscious beauty of Fours.

A calm and stoic Three may experience terrible loss and not pass on the pain or the blows to others. A Four may experience darkness—sadness, loss, melancholy—and nevertheless reflect the brightness a world away. How? By means of holding the vision of light in darkness. Threes feel that nothing changes for them in the midst of external shifts. But a Four knows that Time and Space do not exist. For a Four, everything repeats *but nothing changes*. That is her healing force. Her example frees others from their self-imposed limits—the result of repetition of routine or expectations. A Three derives her power by being apart from the norm. A Four is always at the center of the web and completely free at the same time.

So it is with Female Tricksters. They bewitch. Lady Rokujo, a key figure in one of the most famous medieval tales of love and power ever written, *The Book of Genji*, is an older woman with whom the dashing young prince Genji falls hopelessly in love. Rokujo's love for Genji is so strong that her voice alone has power over him. He hears it when he makes love to his young wife. Rokujo's voice soon takes possession of the young wife. Her presence dispossesses the souls of his other women: when Genji looks at his wife, it is Lady Rokujo's face he sees; he becomes haunted. A Trickster Four disturbs others by threatening to break them of their routine; to disrupt the cycle of whatever repetition in which they might be stuck, and to show them a world as strange and magical as their own. A penetrating beauty creates a deep kind of impact. This is how a mature Four woman makes others pregnant.

A real-life Lady Rokujo was the twentieth-century philosopher Ayn Rand, the imposing author of *The Fountainhead* and *Atlas Shrugged*. Rand's fiction started a cult of political and cultural leaders. Among her acolytes is the brilliant former Federal Reserve chairman Alan Greenspan and countless Fortune 500 executives enamored of Rand's free-market ideas. At age fifty Rand imposed her own face on twenty-four-year-old Nathaniel Branden's brand new wife, Barbara, haunting him as Lady Rokujo possessed Genji. Ayn seduced the young Branden not at a weak moment in his life but one short year after his honeymoon with his beautiful bride. Ayn had real Four juju.

What a Four merely imagines for herself comes into being for others. This sounds like Fours negotiate with the devil, but they are really negotiating with the forces of Creation.

Like Lady Rokujo, Fours appear to create their own fate. Four doctors say they have "a white cloud" overhead in that they experience fewer emergencies on their shifts. It may be that they don't notice the rigors as much, or the fact that they don't put any energy into resisting these rigors.

At the times she rose to the level of a Four, Colette imagined and wrote about a young man who fell in love with an older woman much like herself. She named this character Cherie. Within a year, Colette met the real Cherie: Bertrand de Jouvenal. Had she not imagined Cherie—the sun in her midnight world of an uninspired marriage—would she have encountered her boy lover in the flesh? And when that relationship dissolved in the boy's lasting adoration of Colette, waiting for her in the wings was marriage to a devoted young man who had read her novels at age fourteen.

Such women seem to be everywhere at once; like Tricksters, Eleanor Roosevelt seemed to operate in three time zones at once. She moved with speed but also ease from problem to problem, which she tackled with complete confidence of resolving in some way or other. Time seemed to melt under Eleanor's watch. And when Time melts, Space too becomes more manageable. So with Colette, who seemed young, old, every age available to the power of her self-expression.

A Four accomplishes her big agenda by imagining light in darkness—not one or the other but both. Mother Teresa kissed lepers, seeing the light of grace in their lesion-scarred faces. The philosopher Hannah Arendt was grateful that there were not Holocausts everywhere, when she was immersed in studying the blistering impact of the Nazis on the Jews throughout Europe. Such a peak of maturity is ageless and timeless.

At their very peak of development Tricksters do something unexpected: they *descend* the ladder of command. Because they are without boundaries, Fours wear every one of the faces. They even go below the level of Ones to revert to princessa behavior when necessary, which means they reacquire the qualities of fight and of will (rather than mature submission), of confrontation and resistance. Princessa habits are compelling for the mature when mediated by the fullness of Fours.

Silke Maier-Witt was a notorious young radical in the German Baader-Meinhof Group, which in the 1960s set out to dismantle "evil" capitalism by assassinating members of Germany's economic elite. "Postman" for the group, Maier-Witt transported guns and secret messages throughout eastern Europe until she was captured. When she emerged from prison in her fifties, she shed her idealistic and radical persona and gave herself a new job: that of bringing aid and comfort to widows in the war-torn villages of Kosovo, traveling many of the same back roads she traveled as a youth, but this time not to foment trauma but to heal unrest and upset. She regularly visits villages whose remaining populations of widows are starved for work and funds. She brings them both, teaching them how to rebuild their lives by starting small businesses (the conversion of a Two), acting with neutral aplomb toward her own disrupted past (the stoic Three), yet still in command of princessa-like tactics—evading the factions of Serbs and Croats. Fours, let it be said, are not only their most evolved as ethereal creatures. They are also the hardiest generals in the confrontation against Time.

Maier-Witt never speaks about her past—she is silent as a portrait; but her past caught up with her and has become the stuff of legend in Kosovo. When situations demand, a Four returns to her warrior princessa ways, fighting when necessary.

*   *   *

The remaining six tactics bring the mature woman's presence into greater focus, making her a figure who evokes a big story, not just of her own life's tale but of the story of Life, Death, and Continuity.

A liberal in thought, an autocrat in action,
prudish in words, unbridled in deeds: this is
the recipe for the leader who would submit
like a girl and dominate like a woman.

Youthful sexuality often stands in the way of being taken seriously, and the years after forty-five may be the first time a woman is seen, heard, and appreciated for who she really is. Many believe that a woman may reach a pinnacle—like the presidency of the United States—only when she is of an age beyond erotic appeal. Know that there is no such age. A woman is never beyond erotic appeal. She only becomes more inspirationally or dangerously feminine with age. To put it another way, you do not need feminine wiles when you *are* feminine wiles, when, that is, you have grown into the role of Woman.

Leonardo expressed this in his immortal woman:

there is in the Mona Lisa an absence of common sensuality that makes one pause and shiver, like a sudden wave of cold air in a beautiful building. Her smile contains something worldly, watchful, and self-satisfied. *The love she projects is warm and cold, a kind of eros new to women and more profoundly given in maturity than in youth.* Youthful sexuality ends only in the sense that it yields to mature sexuality, which is not distracting and is more persuasive than any qualities of youth.

This is the fifth law of counterclockwise Time:

A person can be loved thoroughly or transformatively only by an older woman.

A woman becomes complete, strong, and utterly sovereign in her chosen, female domain, and contemptuous of love's frivolity and servitude when she displays such cool eros. In age, one becomes a person and a woman both.

A woman of mature power channels her erotic nature into a force exquisitely primal. She combines a young woman's weakness for commitment and bondage with an old woman's genius for domination. Insatiable and untrusting both, she becomes a dispenser of warmth, fullness, beauty, and pleasure. She needs neither a great heart nor a great mind; yet she requires plaintive nerves, nostrils open to everything, and a magic voice. *She forms an erotic galaxy of mother, lover, and child.* It is her defense against being invisible or negated. That is what makes her so attractive.

The chronicler of mythic leadership, T. H. White, noted that "It is the mother's not the lover's passion that captures the mind. Jocasta, not Juliet, occupies the inner chamber. Gertrude, not the silly Ophelia, who drives Hamlet. Any flirty girl can steal a heart. But a woman who conjures up the figure of the mother, that man exists for her." And not only men, but women, children, and multitudes.

With an older woman, all admirers become young again. They become as children. That is our gift to them. They step out of Time along with us. As the embodiment of cool eros, we will not bear their babies; we bear their youth. We initiate them into a new world.

More people wanted to sit upon the lap of Margaret Mead at the height of her power than thought of her erotically. She had achieved fame not because she was a great thinker, *but because she was so open to everyone and everything.* What people responded to was her energy, her ability to make the most of everything that came her way, hurricanes, volcanoes, even death. They felt protected by Mead, sheltered by her long reach as if she were the flesh-and-blood equivalent of Madonna icons whose long arms encircled crowds and drew them close to her bosom.

Maturity is a healing when one creates a sense for others that they may be mothered again—symbolizing an act of regression and something powerful, a psychologically incestuous act. This is what made the Sun King happy to lie in Madame de Maintenon's arms. This is what Isak Dinesen and Ayn Rand promised their young lovers as well as their admirers; it is what strong female politicians promise their electorate: *to give them a way to return to their origins, to their childhood, when everything was possible.*

The definition of maturity: to recognize the multitude of forms in which love may touch you. Cool eros is one of the most potent and least explored.

From ancient times to modern, men have considered it universally true that they would marry their mothers if the mothers had a face-lift and could have their babies. Folktales from all over the world have a story in which a mother-in-law finds a discarded skin of a young girl, puts it on, and when her son-in-law returns from hunting, he makes love to her and neglects his wife.

If mothers were to cast off—lift—their skins, sons would want their mothers for their wives—hence mothers must die or move away. Die, because mature women lure boys, men, women, crowds, into a desire for experience *that is deeper and richer than procreation.*

A young woman can never appreciate the extent

to which a person's deepest desire is not merely to be happy, warm, or fed, or even to be *one*, as in the sexual act. Rather a person's deepest desire is to be *two* against the world, like an infant in its mother's arms.

Maternal feeling combined with desire—eros—stimulates qualities of regression and renewal: the "child" relaxes into being cared for *and* provoked into his or her maturity.

It is a reversal, a means of sending Time into a retreat. Georgia O'Keeffe decided to do for the young potter Juan Hamilton what her much older husband, Alfred Stieglitz, had done for her in her youth: teach, inspire, and help him craft a career. Juan had come to Ghost Ranch to help with odd jobs, and he stayed with O'Keeffe for the rest of her life, until her death at age ninety-eight.

When they met, she was eighty-six, Juan twenty-eight. She became sweeter and more feminine with him than at any time before in her long life. She began to wear colors: turquoise, maroon, dark green. Their relationship consisted of many elements: man-woman, parent-child, artist-artist. "Juan's the son she never had, and the lover she repressed the need for." What he really needed, Hamilton observed, was a twenty-three-year-old Georgia O'Keeffe.

It is one of the oldest secrets of mature time. The ancient Greek poet Sappho identified herself in youth with the figure of the old woman, inspired by the story of the goddess Aphrodite, disguised as an old woman, who is ferried across a river. On the other side, Aphrodite changes back into a beautiful young goddess who confers beauty and youth on her boatswain as well. But the old woman was the lure. There are heartstrings only a maternal figure can tug.

To Connect Through Cool Eros Is to Employ Female Stoicism, Not Seduction

Promise, implicitly or explicitly, to mother another, and the offer will be grabbed as if by hungry infants.

There is not enough mothering in the world, not from parents, friends, or institutions. Gustave Flaubert, forty-two, confessed to George Sand, fifty-nine, the far more successful writer, that he was "sorely tempted to kiss her like a big child." Never did two people fall more deeply into Platonic love or cool eros. Passionate. Complete. Equal. Not all relationships locked together by cool eros are sexless, but theirs was and lasted for decades with great kindness, mentoring, and devotion.

Do not be subtle in making this promise to be coolly erotic. It draws upon a timeless understanding of what others really need in love: if we come to the point where one may be like a mother *and* a lover to another, that is maturity. It is our loss that except in rare situations, one cannot trip that wire and love a single person both parentally and amorously without contradiction. Cool eros is one of the most mature forms of love to give and to be given.

To consolidate power, tell a new story of connection.

The mature treat love and sex as a subject, not as an effect. A mature woman does not, in other words, set out to conjure a sexual response; *she makes sex her topic.* That is the chill: to make others fall in love with you, instruct them in the topic of love . . . Rand insisted that her young admirer become her lover. Only then, she said, would her teaching about freedom be true to its potential. And yet it was the teaching about love and sexual freedom that drew her lover more than the act.

Madame Recamier would lie down and speak about love. Gertrude Stein gathered artists around her and spoke about love. Cicely Saunders tended the dying speaking about and administering love. So the bettering chill distances eros. Female politicians who speak about love win over electorates in the long run. They come to be respected for expressing emotions few male politicians are brave enough to express.

Use the senses you seldom use in professional life.

Margaret Mead said the ideal society (or circle) would consist of people who were homosexual in their youth and again in old age and heterosexual in the middle of their lives. "What is new is not bisexuality," she wrote, "but rather the widening of our awareness and acceptance of human capacities for sexual love." Mead fell in love with women's souls and men's bodies. She was spiritually homosexual, psychologically bisexual, and physically heterosexual. She wanted people to think there were many more of these affairs than there actually were. "In our culture," she said, "it's good to have the image of the sacred whore." This is particularly true when a woman seeks power in the public arena, where she is judged by her membership in The Three H's: Hair, Hemline, and Husband. To concoct an image that defies all three, as the sacred whore does, earns one a voice.

When Ellen Johnson-Sirleaf won the presidency of Liberia in 2006, she became the first democratically elected female head of state in Africa, ousting warlords whose years of control had decimated the country and plundered its economy. Enemies and friends began calling her "my mother, my sister." She refers to herself as a technocrat—a Harvard-trained economist. "But in Liberia her image is also imbued with a passionate, and at times fetishistic, spiritualism. She is called the Mother of Liberia. . . . She is also called the Iron Lady." She enters a room dressed in brocaded fabrics, covered in bling. She is maternal warmth and unexpected sexuality.

*Forget about compromise and sharing; those days
are over.*

To the mature, "Man has finally been shorn of his magical and commanding force; he no longer either bars doors or opens them." Mature women do not crave the paternalistic in men. Rather, the boyish in men makes them attractive to mature women.

Young men were drawn to Colette after age fifty even more than when she was young in large part because she could be coldly unforgiving of her lovers, demanding like a mother: "I sometimes forget an insult but never a kindness." That "sometimes" put people on notice.

Having lost their childhood, most are searching to recover it. Know that your admirers and lovers—particularly the young—are noble figures willing to be ruled by love. A young person's idleness, passivity, weakness, puerility, and inability to adapt constitute a noble revolt against modernity. Such young people "[back] away, with an unspeakable repugnance, from the idea of living...in a world no longer ruled by love." There are many "young souls" who are forever caught in a form of infancy; they are eager to join with you in your purpose.

Goethe ends *Faust*, his tale of the seeker who tries everything only to succeed at last by coming to this understanding in, appropriately, the Kingdom of the

Mothers: "The Eternal Feminine draws us on," promising that all will live their unlived lives and thereby regenerate themselves.

Await your lost children. Knowing the power of cool eros will awaken the desire for it in others.

Add to a motherly, sisterly, wifely tone of "We who forbade" a loving "We who enjoy." In so doing, you experience more pleasure and share it.

"We who enjoy" expresses the force of gallantry. Courtliness in behavior to one's liege expands the pleasure of the unequal relationship. A mature woman may be intimidating because she is so far beyond most others in thinking and in ability to act, should she choose to do so. She may deflect others' fears by communicating as the mother-sister-wife in frequent thank-yous to others. She suggests a coy taking of blame for what goes wrong. A half-ironic statement—"Oh, I am such a foolish old woman"—is a subtle reminder of her difference, and difference in mature relationships is the invitation to pleasure, not the thing to avoid.

To gain pleasures, a woman must make herself infinitely more susceptible to pleasure.

A change in tone from self-sacrificing youth to pleasure-seeking and enjoying requires not will or action but the cultivation of submission and abandonment.

Submission is a discipline, and the only one that opens a person up to love of the vast kind: an almost religious ecstasy.

The arts of submission are a mature woman's greatest friend. They may be practiced, not as in inequality or submission to another, but as submission to joy.

"A woman reaches an age when the only thing left to her is to enrich her own self," said Colette. Physical pleasure can overcome the worst grief. To become better at experiencing pleasure is to divest oneself of the romantic myth of love that is hot and everlasting, and to seek pleasure in cold love. Women in their maturity feel free at last to love as men typically love, for pleasure.

Pleasure depends on that which cannot be contained, which bursts boundaries, rendering the center—the safe, harmless center—nowhere at all. It disrupts the dominant or traditional structure of power. Accepting pleasure (rather than pleasing) is a heroic act.

It is possible to be commanding at eighty or ninety if one never tires of pleasure. "Show me a dandy and I'll show you a hero," Baudelaire said. "Who would think, to look at me, and considering my peaceful old age, that I still dote on excess?" George Sand confessed to Flaubert. From age forty-eight until she died at age seventy-one, she had, in addition to her Platonic lover Flaubert, half a dozen long-term sexual affairs with young lovers, one after the other.

Louise Nevelson attracted many admirers because of her talent for pleasure. She would sign off long conversations with "We've had a wonderful time so far, but I think *this* year, we're *really* going to have a good time." Her good-byes were sometimes "Be sexy with me." Her hellos were "Words, is that all you've got?" Pleasure was always first in her talk.

"My life gets richer every day," Nevelson explained at age eighty about the combination of pleasure with an ascetic work schedule. Her hours in her studio were a daily rebirth in a heightened state. By her eighty-fourth year she was radiant and beautiful, said one observer. "When you're my age," she said, "all you have is your life."

The pleasure of mature love has little to do with lust and much to do with impossible goals.

Saints, so-called ascetics, are the greatest models of mature love. They are epicures of cool eros and engage in practices of remarkably subservient delight. Ascetics want pleasure that is both intense and constant and runs all through the body. They are enraptured by impossible goals. They want to be flooded with love. They want a vessel into which they may pour themselves. Saint Teresa, in the sculptor Brunelleschi's rendering, leans back flooded with pleasure that is so spiritual, it electrifies her whole body.

So think of yourself as a saint: Ascetic life is not, historically, the denial of pleasure but *a new strategizing of pleasure*—a mode of caring for oneself, surpassing or transcending oneself, or as Nietzsche put it, "self-overcoming," meaning overcoming one's ordinary notion of what pleasure is and where it may begin.

The unspoken pact between those who love like a mother and their beloveds is that the master-parent— the mature person—will hold on for both of them.

When an older woman admits her love for anyone younger, that youth is on his way to being lost. One must invite the love, show or express the love, and nurture it, but not declare it. Bertrand de Jouvenal, at sixteen, was deeply in love with Colette, but she would wait until their affair was almost over—nearly five years later—to tell the boy explicitly that she loved him. The bond itself must remain unconscious.

These young beloveds and admirers may behave from time to time like spoiled children and wicked nurslings. As such, they love to hear that a master-parent blames herself for anything that goes wrong. Then they forget their level of enslavement: Colette's alter ego Lea tells her young lover Cheri, "Had I really been cool, I should have made a man of you and not thought only of the pleasures of your body and my own happiness. My darling, I am to blame for everything you lack." Do not fear being the one to apologize. It is a display of strength and increases the bond you share with those who seek mothering.

*To be maternal to an electorate or a community
requires that one have the soul of Brutus, the betrayer,
and the charms of Cleopatra, the lover.*

This was the tactic of Mother Russia, as Catherine the Great worked to become: a legend in her own time, unquestioned for her stand. Unlike Elizabeth I, Empress Catherine was less interested in the brilliant societal trappings of power than in its inner workings, and these yielded to her cool eros style of governance. Catherine brought a lamp and a broom to her display of power. She bent tirelessly over reports, memoranda, diplomatic correspondence, and national accounts. She felt that paperwork was the hidden but essential part of the job of ruling. When no one could tell her the size of the Russia she ruled, she asked for a map to count the territories inside its borders. But there was no map of Russia in the Senate archives, so with a smile she gave five rubles to a young officer and told him to buy a copy at the Academy of Sciences. In everything, she assumed she was governing children, but children she greatly respected.

She loved Russia's faults even as she swore to reform them and betray or stand against tradition. For a person who worshipped clarity, Catherine was greatly tempted to straighten out Russia's childish messes: the empire was pulled in dozens of directions and everything was based on custom that often contradicted itself. She thought the Russians were a great and beautiful people, and loved them as her children. She took seriously the title "Little Mother" and wanted to be a source of warmth to the people. She was also spiritually seductive: her mind had been trained from youth by reading Montesquieu and Voltaire and she easily dominated visiting dignitaries, using all she knew as a form of flirtation.

All her life Catherine worked at building her own legend. In the years after age forty-five, she knew exactly what she wanted and had the stature to get it. People who met her expected her to be as tall as her legend.

She found a father figure to join her, but not as an equal; no one contested the power of the great mother. Late in life, Catherine fell in love for the first time with the magician Potemkin, whom his friends called "one-eyed and ripe-smelling." The two worked the country until it became an empire. Countries were annexed, threats—like Turkey—annihilated.

She encouraged profound thoughts and childish follies in those closest to her. Being bored was a contagion. After she was forty-five, all her lovers were younger than she. They were virtually identical: she was in pursuit of the ideal companion and considered that the image of her soul would be found only in the "army" of young men she loved—"grandsons," she called them—to carry out her legacy.

Throughout her reign, Catherine grew greater than even her nation. Having come to Russia as a little German princess, she had not only learned Russian and changed her religion; she had adopted the soul of her new country. She wanted to be the incarnation of Russia though she hadn't a drop of Russian blood in her veins. This may be her most extraordinary achievement. At her death, the nation did not call her Catherine the Great but Little Mother Catherine.

You cannot use the word "love" too often.

But the love of which we speak is not romantic love; it is a love that is as inclusive as friendship. It is not based on longing but on loving what you have. Use the word "love" often in public, in private, in politics, and in pleasure. Speaking it evokes love in others. The word creates a safe space in which people may submit to each other's desires and aims. Be your most captivating, but realize that if you try to determine the outcome in anything, but especially in love, success will be difficult. You are not a princessa anymore; you are a Teacher and a Stoic, with hopes of becoming as large of outlook as a country. Do not therefore grow angry with a lover's ambivalence or rejection. You have no control over what happens and whatever happens will be to your benefit, even if—especially if—loss is involved. This is submission to love, not to a beloved.

Princessas learned to resist negative forces. But only mature leaders may submit to them because only a mature woman knows how powerful it is to play at love. Learning to submit is one of the prodigies of maturity.

TACTIC 6

The body is subject to the forces of gravity.
But the soul is ruled by levity. Master the depths
of your mysterious smile, because a woman's
laughter is more powerful than her tears.

Like Christ and all other amazing people, a woman
who fascinates has the power of not merely saying
beautiful things but of making other people say beautiful things to her.

That, Madame de Lafayette knew, requires one take
the nastiest comments in the most playful way and
express them playfully too: see everything as amusing
and return assaults in the same exact manner. *When one
smiles, one creates, for a time, equals. Complicity. Allies!*—
because only equals may laugh.

A smile communicates pleasure and so degrades opposing power. The Mona Lisa's iconic smile is like the
faces of very old women: they smile knowingly. A slight

smile is altogether a serious matter: it overcomes barriers of timeworn habit, routine, and prejudice. Glance away from the Mona Lisa's mouth and see a serious face in the form of sad, searching eyes. She flickers between deep dark intent and surprising wit—a combination of seriousness and humor. A suggestion of lordly amusement plays about her face.

What a kiss is to the Godfather—bestowed on another, it says, "I own you"—a smile is to a Godmother. The smile says welcome to my world . . . I own a piece of you, the best of you.

The gods are always laughing. When a woman laughs she is engaged in a godly pursuit: she is remaking the troubled world into a golden world of laughter. In such a vision, impossible things cannot happen but do happen. We know that a young boy cannot possibly fall in love with an older woman . . . but in comedy he does exactly this. We know that a woman who acts as a great man cannot change the course of politics, yet using comic timing, she does so. We know that fall is fall and spring, spring, but in comedies fall and spring exist together in charmed landscapes. Things that are too good to be true are real in comic time. With comic insight and timing, we may transform Time—notice that each of these examples overturns the usual sequence of events. Sadness and tragedies unfold in real Time, when one is a prisoner of Time. But comedies end up in a golden Time, when everyone is happy ever after.

True female heroism involves a special kind of healing: in returning people to a point where happy endings prevail. In age, the most power one has is in becoming a comedic heroine and using the timing genius of great comediennes. One does not ordinarily think of the comic as heroic; one thinks that tragic heroines arise in tragedies and bravely endure shattered lives. But the elements of comedy contain the ultimate heroine story. As they say in Hollywood, the kid dies but it's all to the good, to redeem the world. Who is this hero but Christ or Moses who from a journey of suffering comes to the edge of the Holy Land? The comedic heroine delivers people to a vision of paradise where nothing goes wrong for long. Spiritual life is the sweetest comedy of all.

To create a golden world, one must arrive at maturity, for the mature woman has seen too much and knows the limits of the rational world. Instead she puts her faith in the mysterious personal force that commands: things happen, of course—people get sick, they get lost, they make money and lose it. To the mature woman, however, these are non-events because she does not think "tragedy." She knows that tragic heroines use suffering. They use it to grow stronger. By contrast the comedic heroine lives with suffering in anticipation of the day when release from suffering occurs.

The gods look upon mortal follies and laugh. Take your place, for a time, among them.

The smile and the laughter know no inhibitions, no limitations. They possess the most natural magic of all, overturning logic just enough so that miracles become possible. They silence violence and shatter resistance.

To create this golden world, one must transport people from illusion to reality, from habit or ritual bondage to freedom.

Optimism Is Your Means of Resistance

Princessas are so serious. But in the Mona Lisa world, the slight smile guides us: meet threats with optimism. Lightness of treatment rejects all heaviness. Consider the criticisms leveled at First Lady Hillary Clinton, age forty-five, advocating a national health care program in 1991. The anger she evoked was much the same as the criticism leveled six decades earlier against Eleanor Roosevelt, just turning fifty, urging social security legislation upon her husband, President Franklin Delano Roosevelt, in the years before he finally enacted these benefits in 1935. Today men advocate similar agendas to great applause. But women who make sweeping statements risk being ignored and attacked. It is enough to convince us that biographies of women should begin not with their birth but rather with the moment when girls learn they are not boys and lack the freedoms men have to say what they think, in completely straight-forward language or heartfelt oratory. *That* is when women are born. Until the public welcomes women's messages in women's voices, another voice must step in the breach of heroism. The option is to put one's messages across by evoking laughter.

The Danish writer Karen Blixen took, in her late forties, to signing her work "Isak" (coupled with her maiden surname, Dinesen). *Isak* in Hebrew means "the one who laughs." Isak was the child of Abraham and Sarah's extreme old age—a postmenopausal miracle, a divine joke. Despair over having lost her farm and her lover in Africa made Blixen a writer. That loss gave her a second life *was best understood as a joke, and "God loves a joke" became her maxim in the latter part of her life.*

Join the Presiding Queens of Laughter

Women we think of as serious have risen to iconic stature on a streak of comedy. Maureen Dowd affects a half-smile to challenge the social and political hierarchy. The most successful actresses began in comedy and moved to drama: Katharine Hepburn, Reese Witherspoon, Julia Roberts, and Mary Tyler Moore.

The mature in positions of power are bravest in their use of the comic: former secretary of state Madeleine Albright wore amusingly ironic pins in meetings with high diplomats. When she had a high-level meeting with a diplomat from a country in which aid was not reaching the poor, she wore a Daddy Warbucks brooch to mock the poor record of the diplomat. The marketing guru Faith Popcorn sells ultra-serious consumer research in the guise of a clown with spiky hair, a comic name, and a wry smile. The artist Louise Bourgeois wears a dress of forty breasts like the send-up of an ancient statue of the earth mother. Suze Orman delivers sound financial advice in a Phyllis Diller shriek. Emily Dickinson may have been a recluse but she was foremost a supreme wit, teasing her friend Thomas Wentworth Higginson, calling him the Master while pulling him along by the nose. Colette toyed with her young followers. Joan Didion in her late middle years became a serious political commentator in a voice of bone-dry irony.

Promise to live happily ever after.

A humorous touch promises others a return to a state of newfound happiness after a tumultuous beginning. You may make this promise and reach a state of peace because although you are increasingly open to fate, you become invulnerable to its traumas.

Colette lived her life as if it were a comedy, not a tragedy. At fifty she attained the happiest years of her life—she married her second husband at fifty-two and wrote her most famous books. That thrill lasted until she reached sixty, when she surpassed happiness and reached the height of her glory, writing more easily than ever and marrying a boy half her age who took exquisite care of her. That is comedic heroism.

Forget funny.

A funny person is funny only for so long. But a woman of wit can be spellbinding forever. Spark laughter sometimes, but to make others quiet and to make them marvel—is to use the half-smile. Speak the truth to power lightly. Truth is what people want although it frightens them.

To be cool and calm is to be humorous.

A sense of humor is a very stable thing. When you are serious, you could be unstable, ready at a moment's notice to burst into tears or recrimination. That's the problem with seriousness.

Aim your amusement at yourself.

The chief weapon of heroic humor is the moral penetration of *irony* and *self-parody*, which are felt as delight. Do not critique others but aim it at oneself as example. Youth tries always to be serious, especially about one's promise or value to a company or to others. In maturity, this makes one seem dour and spent. Julia Child became a household icon in her fifties by creating of herself the figure of a major woman television comic second only to Carol Burnett and Lucille Ball. Child was a serious chef, but her means of communicating were highly comic. Emptying a bottle of cabernet into a stew, hacking a chicken like a campy *Sweeney Todd* murderess, were the outward techniques of a serious woman who served the art of cooking.

Child was dead serious about her art and her reputation, but she began the fashion of public chefs as clowns. She made the mission of cooking so pleasurable that it drew hundreds of students, worshippers, and admirers to her and led her husband, Paul, to abandon his career to manage hers. It is difficult to imagine Child becoming so powerful without this smiling heroism.

Insouciance buys a woman vast leverage over seriousness. *Playfulness* forestalls backsliding into the world of anxious interest and selfish solicitude—the domain of Ones, and to a lesser extent, of Twos. To mock oneself does not come easily to Ones and Twos. Prestige and appearance take precedence over self-irony. Threes and Fours are more experimental and less dependent on appearance.

Talk faster, and change subjects abruptly.

Former *Vogue* editor Diana Vreeland described the actor Clark Gable in teasing terms:

I wish I could give you a load of his eyelashes. He had the most beautiful eyelashes I've ever seen on a man—on a human being. They were exactly like a Shetland pony's. Now you're probably not as intimate with Shetland ponies as I am. They're terrible little beasts—but they have the longest, fuzziest eyelashes of any creature you've ever seen. Clark's were exactly like that.

Rapidly and repeatedly changing the subject, from Gable to eyelashes to ponies, makes people gawk, and then they laugh. Speed up your conversation and you change the nature of Time. You are perceived differently. The tone may go from serious to sentimental to angry but then back to light, winning you new allies in your golden vision. Vreeland makes the teasing gentle. She makes Gable seem a close and intimate confederate in the tone she takes. By comparing him to a pony, she does him a favor: she makes him even more lovable, and able to laugh at himself. And what she does to her own image—so discreetly—is the most interesting of all. She positions herself as the divinely amused observer of Gable. She does not complain about him, she does not worship him: she positions herself as if on a throne, very like the Mona Lisa, looking down, completely amused, so lordly . . .

The classic change-up: switch the traditional, and you have the situation on its knees.

When the poet Robert Lowell attended a birthday party for the prematurely mature Jackie Kennedy in 1996, he remarked upon her ease among the powerful. She insisted on introducing him to Defense Secretary Robert McNamara, putting her hand over Lowell's mouth and telling him to be polite. "I [was] saying something awkward about liking him but not his policy," because McNamara was responsible for the increasing deaths in Vietnam. Jackie replied to Lowell, "How impossibly banal. You should say you adore his policy but find him dull." Jackie, so mature, so young: no wonder she became the center of all attention with her reality-changing wit.

Margaret Mead once took the floor at a contentious meeting and talked about the pecking order of chickens. The audience, expecting a serious discourse, was astonished and listening intently. They gradually discerned that Mead's figure of speech was code for them, the members of the audience, and they began to giggle, then to laugh, and then to applaud. Mead would often follow a compliment by a probe. She would turn things around: once while talking to a Fragrance Foundation honcho she asked what he was doing to people "by blurring their sense of smell."

Abrupt change-ups turn existing authority upside

down, play up absurd coincidences, or use stagey expressions of feeling (like Vreeland on eyelashes). People look at the established power on his high-horse and see only a bore. They would rather throw their lot in with you. Such is the coin of influence.

A woman resists bores, attacks, and the threat of invisibility with optimism.

This is because playfulness is a victory of the pleasure principle. Pleasure is the most subversive force in history.

Provoke laughter at something and its horror dissolves. Our power regenerates with shared laughter. *Pleasure and play shatter the limits of the rational world.* With it we create the belief that one can cope with a future fraught with dangers and opportunities, and that these perils are merely coincidences, nothing more.

"Nothing bores or troubles me in a world where . . . as far as I'm concerned, all is for the best," wrote George Sand.

Include rather than exclude people into your society.

Tragedy leaves no one standing at the end. Comedy welcomes everyone onto the stage. The more people you invite into your golden vision, the better the chance for humor to flourish.

Mark your enemies not as the villainous but as the judgmental.

Those who judge you will never be your closest supporters. To win them over is impossible.

Reverse hidebound rules and thereby create a golden age.

Mute any power that doesn't have a playful streak. Princessas seek to alter the social hierarchy; the mature do not. In the mature mind, kings remain kings and clowns remain clowns; only the personal relationships within society are altered. For example, clowns see truth more clearly. They can speak their minds freely. As such, they have more power than kings.

The magic is in metamorphosis: order is turned upside down but it is still order. A political Camelot, which Jackie Kennedy appeared to have invented of her husband's presidency, was every bit as odd and even silly a place as Julia's kitchen: a government assumed to be run like King Arthur's Round Table? But the mere suggestion of both put the conventional order on notice that things could be very different. Princessas had to actively defy the social order to achieve their ends. No wonder they were as vulnerable as sparrows. In the Mona world, where less is more, a smile is worth ten battles. Women's power in maturity is seldom the result of fighting or joining Power Central, but of standing just slightly apart from it with a knowing smile.

Expect a happy ending. But not a Cinderella ending.

There is no gratification of fantasy here. A comedic heroine's dreams are realer than real. This is her happy ending. A marriage at the end of a comedy is the kind of thing that cannot happen, yet we see it happening. Young men losing their hearts to women twice their age cannot happen, yet it does. Coco Chanel reconquering the fashion world at age seventy with old designs cannot happen, yet it does. Death is the inevitable result of birth. But *new life* is not the inevitable result of death—and out of ashes and trouble, a laugh may ensue. New life is always coming out of a comedic view of reality. Renewal depends on faith, hope, and love, which are not rational virtues.

Do not act or react to everything. React and you force another's hand. Drama builds. Tragedy may ensue.

If you stop acting, you will be able to effect an aesthetic change. *Action builds to a head, comedy to a resolution.* Let things unfold without intervention. Make sure your *manners* and *attitudes* are right; these are more important than *morals* and *actions*—and you thereby dissipate your anxieties and others.

A comedic heroine evokes sympathy and pleasure. Her purpose is to reveal something wisdom doesn't see, like new self-knowledge or a release from mechanical form of repetitive behavior. Wit is a light shed on routine. A comic's wit leads to self-knowledge that is freeing. It is not introverted knowledge, but knowledge about the world and how it works. A commentary on eyelashes takes all the air out of pretentiousness, which is traditional power. Comic heroines are masters at shifting from an action world, dominated by men and power, to a world of re-reflection, wherein things look different.

Strike a tone of the "light rhythm" of life; and know that the reason it is "light" is that all creatures love life.

"When you know when to laugh and when to look upon things as too absurd to take seriously, the other person is ashamed to carry through even if he was serious about it." Eleanor Roosevelt, at age sixty-one, said this of her strategy with the antagonistic Russians. "In some ways they are more like us than [our allies] the British. They will joke about things Mr. Churchill considers sacred. He takes them deadly seriously and argues with them when what he ought to do is laugh."

Play at love and *experience its depths at the same time.*

A person with a tragic view of the world has a deep and secret fear: she believes that an error from her past will come back to haunt her if she dares show pride in herself. Think of all the tragic heroes, from Oedipus, who was told early in life that he would bring about the downfall of his kingdom of Thebes; or King Arthur, who made a political decision early in life that he was warned would destroy all of Camelot; to Jane Eyre, who believed her sad childhood set her up for a tragic adulthood. Comediennes, by contrast, have amnesty from their pasts. They alone may re-create themselves free of suffering. The past has no claim upon them. It is ripe; it drops away; they are free. A comedic heroine thus awakens from loss to gain. She does not put stock in guilt. She experiences rebirth, a renewal of the powers of nature. A Renaissance.

The comedic heroine Emily Dickinson did not have any special interest in her past nor a great deal of concern about her future. Her life was lived in moments.

Inebriate of Air—am I—
And Debauchee of Dew—
Reeling—thro endless summer days—
From inns of Molten Blue—

When "Landlords" turn the drunken Bee
Out of Foxglove's door—
When Butterflies—renounce their "drams"—
I shall but drink the more!

Consider that your life unfolds not as one story but rather in unconnected episodes.

One acquires more experimental capacity when one sees one's life as a collection of episodes that may or may not be connected, or if connected, then by a comic thread. The idea that our lives are narratives puts undue emphasis on striving for boring consistency. The better a person is at submitting to fate's circuitous path, the more love and adventure enter into her life. Golda Meir's life was high comedy although it was lived amid war, loss, and tragedy. Her life unfolded in episodes; the ironies, not the tragedies, stood out: the irony of a Milwaukee housewife becoming a farmer in the desert, of all places, then a warrior fighting for and defending her country, is ridiculous. It couldn't happen, but it did. Meir kept up a steady pace of ironic humor in her public messages, even when losses became intolerable: Menachem Begin said, "Golda Meir, the earth mother!—you throw yourself on her bosom and the next minute you're dead." To which she replied, "The last time someone threw himself on my bosom I'm too old to remember, but they didn't act dead." Notice her skill at changing the subject of Death to Love. Notice her wit in turning self-deprecation into a declaration of overcoming: her ability to thwart Begin's nastiness. She offered a new order, as when she made her most ardent comment about the future: "There will be peace when the Arabs learn to love their children *more* than they hate the Jews." For her, irony was a strategy, a provocation that is half humorous, teasingly serious, with a hope of writing a new ending to an unfolding tragedy.

A heroine-healer at her best is Shakespeare's most mature female character, Rosalind. Reacting to an episode of bad luck that deposes her father from his high position in court, Rosalind flees the court and enters Arden Forest. Leaving the "rational" order, Rosalind comes into her own power in the wilds of Arden. The forest, Shakespeare wishes us to know, is the idea of chaos: a maternal realm, a magic realm, a comic Garden of Eden, *where anything lost is revived as joy.* Here Rosalind may speak her courageous comedy marked by laughter and serious discussion. She establishes that she is a heroine who exists apart from the known, rational order.

In Arden, she meets the wonderful Orlando, whose immaturity she recognizes and doesn't try to minimize. Instead, she remakes him into a man she may love and who may love her as she deserves to be loved.

Rosalind is Shakespeare's Mona Lisa. She is a Four— "the most admirable person in all of Shakespeare," says the scholar Harold Bloom. She is a fictional creation, yes, but Bloom conjectures that she is the female Shakespeare himself longed to become. She is dead serious, yet she speaks truth in language that is not beautiful or full of high dudgeon or the least bit critical in direct terms. Comedy becomes her intricate spiritual choreography. Her strategy in Arden is to disguise herself as a man who is acting the part of a woman—herself. She literally makes herself a man who is all woman. With Orlando, she assumes a voice of cool eros: she patiently, spiritually, and sometimes spankingly teaches him how to love her. And here she trips a wire young women do not dare cross: Rosalind would have Orlando love her like a father *and* like a man, to cherish her freedoms and to love her unconditionally.

She toys with Orlando in her guise as a great man who is all woman: she uses comedic mayhem and mischief not to make herself more important than Orlando but rather for the purpose of maturing Orlando. She means to teach him the nature of conscious love, which is mature love, and so different from the love based on fantasy—the romantic myth. She tells him that no one has ever died from love. She instructs him in simple things, such as that a partner needs to be on time for appointments with her. And she points out that a man must never demean or criticize a woman for speaking her mind in a comic vein, not even when it threatens to turn the world upside down. Mature heroines welcome this task of teaching lovers and admirers, and maturing them into people fit for a world made of love.

Orlando had been in danger of being a bit too comfortable with conventions and how we like it. But Rosalind, in her male disguise, chips away steadily at Orlando's conventional responses until they speak a shared language, their witty dialogue barely concealing a subtext that explores how they imagine what life would be like with each other.

Bloom has said that "no happiness has ever surpassed Rosalind's." She is both an erotic realist and a superbly benign critic of romantic love. She is the closest to a fully realized woman whose female nature includes masculine certainty.

This voice works not only in Arden Forest but in the halls of power.

To undo power, the comedic or mischievous voice restores what is missing in public life.

Former Texas governor Ann Richards delivered her famous 1988 Democratic National Convention address without grandeur or grandiloquence, not profoundly Churchillian in rhetoric, Rooseveltian in promises, or Clintonesque in scholarship. Richards's tone was famously neighborly *and* impish. She began with conventional *storytelling*, then she delivered in all winking wit a line so devastatingly funny about then president George Herbert Walker Bush that it still stings him: she said he was born with "a silver foot in his mouth." One can get away with anything if it is said with a smile and provokes a smile.

* * *

Women are expected to provide a view inside real life, where the shadow holds forth: the dark side of manipulativeness that male politicians seek to ignore. The voice that recognizes the evil in the world, not to hide it or ignore it, but instead give it authentic presence . . . and twist it into a funny balloon creature: this is provocative but it is also inviting and healing. This is the doorway to the golden world, a far better world of one's imagining. To evoke such a world is to gain a confidence in one's own timing, in the force of one's own pleasure to slow down Time, and to beguile others with the beauty of the god's own view of the unchanging and eternal.

Hate and wait, because one doesn't grow
strong on a diet of wimpy burgers. Do not fear
critics or appease them. Rather, bring forth
tigers out of their cocoons.

Let us break the bulletproof glass around Saint
Leonardo's well-behaved woman for a moment and
imagine our Time-defiant heroine out of her bubble in
the Louvre and at large in the real world. How might a
long-patient Mona Lisa—who has seen all kinds of humanity parade before her—react when confronted with
the worst of it? When might her smile curl into a snarl?
This dark chapter in the annals of power takes its title
from the motto of the maligned Catherine de' Medici, an
Italian queen humiliated in the French court into which
she married. Catherine was criticized for being chubby,
plain, and Italian. She hid her weight under robes, and
her secret strategy was similarly cloaked: it was "Odi-

ate et Aspetate," or Hate and Wait. "Caress only your enemies," because friends can stand the truth.

To face evil with grace abounding is not always possible. Catherine felt herself powerless for years against her much older rival for her husband the king's attention, Diane de Poitiers. Diane was a One, a much-admired and long-preserved beauty, and she entwined herself with the king from his boyhood on. A kiss from her at a vulnerable moment in his youth imprinted itself upon him, and he never lost faith in her. She became his advisor, mistress, and eventually mothered the children his wife bore him. He obeyed his duty to propagate his royal line with Catherine—*à la levrette*, like a greyhound, so he would never have to look at her. But it was Diane he slept beside. Catherine drilled a hole in her floor and saw how her husband made love to Diane: "He never used me so well," she said, weeping. And then all at once, upon her husband's untimely death, Catherine unleashed her power. She stripped Diane of the home and much of the wealth and power the king had given her. Catherine had spent years sharing her husband and her role as queen with Diane. Widowhood alone would be hers. She would learn to fashion history according to her own needs. To do that, she set out to arouse fear, going on the offensive, as queens may do occasionally.

"The older I get, the more convinced I am that you have to be a bit of an asshole to get *anything* accomplished in this world," said Susan Sontag, who achieved recognition and respect in her twenties by honing her talents, friendships, and personality. But to leverage her power in age, to take on the new work of writing novels and mounting plays in war zones like Kosovo, she more than occasionally unleashed a bolt of tyranny and retribution. Women prefer their heroines to be consistently good, but as we expand the definition of femininity, we see that creators must also practice their power as destroyers. One cannot keep turning the other cheek in age without arousing the avenger inside. Simone Weil, who died too young, said the true test of courage is taking a blow and not passing it on; so young princessas believe that they must learn to absorb acts of hatred and not react. But in maturity, one cannot afford to turn abuse inward. One is wise to give as good as you get, and to express extreme anger in a tone of bewitchment, double-talk, and wild irrationality—the comic at its most absurd.

A display of strength is occasionally required to meet attacks of biliousness. When one has attained a high level of power, as for example Fours do, one may only then match force with force. A queen may indulge in such behavior once or twice in a lifetime as a show of pure power. The most beautiful and iconic women have done so: in the prize ring of life, the novelist John Updike said, few would have lasted ten rounds with Colette. Hate only as long as you wait. Once you act, hold nothing back.

Power is, as we have said, an animal instinct. To express it requires knowing how far you can go—and being fearless in the face of your own strength.

Let detractors reckon with you. They must know they hurt you—or impede your mission—at a cost not to you but to themselves. This is the way the world works. To be soft, you must also be more than tough: you must be shrapnel. You must know what you are capable of, and others must know it too. Respect is an unlimited line of credit in the halls of power. If people know you won't take their humiliations, they will deal with you respectfully. Charm takes you farther if people know how far you can go.

It is not easy to be a monster, Colette said. *Or to recognize that in age one is a monster.* "It is even harder than being a saint." Women are monsters, she concludes, and a saint is often a monster of pleasure. Women who have seen this sacred monster in themselves attain the highest precocities of maturity. To show anger with humor is our aim.

> Young men in myth go out and kill the beast.
> Few ask: who is the beast? The answer: the
> aging woman, back with redoubled strength.

In one respect the Stratagem makes a woman more vulnerable to others' manipulations because it encourages her to surrender to larger forces or emotions. But do not even consider submitting or responding in a soulful way when attacked or dissed. Character is made of tempered steel, sharpened and hardened by suffering. A woman will need to administer an occasional dose of stiletto. The acid critics of female politicians throw doubt upon their minds, as when political enemies sought to disparage Elizabeth I as flighty. Not only enemies but lovers, too, humiliate women they idolize: Dashiell Hammett professed his love for the playwright Lillian Hellman, who regularly found him in bed with other women...the Ike Turners of the world cannot be overcome by charm, comedy, patience, or cool eros. They must be unmasked as children.

Edith Wharton's forty-five-year-old life quickened when she met the gadabout Morton Fullerton. She saw Fullerton's weakness, undependability, and philandering. Even after he disappointed her and embarrassed her, she decided not to leave him but to adjust to a new image of him: not the hero of her dreams but the man she loved and who had loved her. How nice, but how powerless a response.

"I never wonder what you are doing when you are not with me," she wrote Fullerton. "At such moments I feel as though all the mysticism in me—the transcendentalism that in other women turns to religion—were poured into my feeling for you, giving me a sense of *immanence*, of inseparableness from you. In one of the moods...when you were reproaching me for never giving you any sign of my love for you, I felt like answering: 'But there is a contact of thought that seems so much closer than a kiss.'"

Her friend Henry James advised her to be gracious. When Fullerton's faithlessness got under her skin and she thought of leaving him, James counseled forgiveness: "I am moved to say, 'Don't *conclude!*' ...Only sit tight yourself and go through the movements of life." In other words, keep an open mind and distract yourself from overthinking the betrayals. "[Doing] such things...the deeper and darker [emotions] stay in their place." Had Wharton met Fullerton's passive-aggressive humiliations with force, he might have respected her and behaved respectfully. Professions of love do not come with hurt. To hate the treatment and accept it by waiting it out condones the action.

Know this about the Fullertons of the world. They are people with whom you cannot build goodwill. No matter what you do for them, they forget it the moment it is done. Nothing adds up because for them the only thing that matters is what you are doing for them in the moment—which they take as a sign that they control you: evidence of your enslavement to their whims. They are the devils of Time, its vilest mercenaries. They use your power and turn you against yourself. The world is too full of them to avoid; you must instead use them. And you must use them in such a way to disable them from hurting others. Because when they finish with you, they will exercise their whims upon others. Kindness and cruelty do not make a dent against them. Instead, laugh at them. They cannot withstand laughter. It punctures their ego.

Betrayal is intolerable in bed or out. Eleanor Roosevelt lamented that in her position as First Lady she would try to sell the men in her husband's cabinet on an idea or a proposal. They would sit opposite her and barely pretend to listen, a blank or distracted look on their faces. When she finished speaking, they would start a conversation that had nothing to do with what she had just said. And so she made end runs around them, filling her cabinet with trusted women friends, and rather than seeking her detractors' advice, she ignored them.

Hate and wait. Ignore opponents until you can ignore them no longer. Then go on the offensive: oppose your antagonist at the most abandoned level of your self-control. Be the equal then of your haters. Know that you can be a sacred monster.

The Winning Paradox of the Entangling Woman

A woman's strength is highly contingent. She depends on many, and many seek to trip her up. The greater her circle of friendship and love, the greater her vulnerability. Penelope, the queen of ancient Ithaca, had a very modern problem. Abandoned by her husband Odysseus for twenty years—he left to fight a war and, victorious, set a leisurely course for home—she governed Ithaca in his absence and raised their son to manhood. After nearly two decades, she was assumed to be widowed and a great many suitors arrived at her palace and sought to marry her, drawn, she feared, not by her charms but by her wealth and position. Her son, concerned about how a new husband could threaten his right to his father's throne, might have sent her away or even killed her. How long before her maids—her closest female allies—would spread lies about her honor to increase their own standing with the supporters of the absent Odysseus? Penelope was vulnerable to those she should have been most able to trust.

> The entangler avoids entanglement.
>
> She alone is free.

She decided to outwit them all. She told the suitors she would not choose a new husband from among them until she had finished weaving a shroud for her aged father-in-law. It was her way of waiting out the crisis. Every day she wove, and every night she secretly undid her weaving. As has been said, the best action is often inaction. The shroud, known as "Penelope's web," has come to refer to any task that remains mysteriously and cleverly—comically—unfinished:

> *I did not appreciate the term web. . . . I had not been attempting to catch men like flies:* on the contrary, I'd merely been trying to avoid entanglement myself.

A weaver of webs is free of entanglements. Penelope's strengths lie in the classic maneuvers of irrational action combined with direct responses. It is a form of going on the offensive while still waiting or appearing to be innocent of vengeful deeds. It works by the following means:

Be strong enough to be stimulated by what shatters others.

Think "bilious." Any effort at character assassination against a woman deserves no less a term. Do not react immediately when you have been treated disrespectfully. Wait a few days, a few hours. Your antagonist will think he's won. Then act. In a meeting arranged by a baron of business with a younger, less influential prince, a powerful woman whose counsel the baron valued was also present. The prince began to point out the woman's flaws, thinking it would raise his standing with the baron to be seen as a cogent critic. The woman remained decorous and polite until the dinner's end, when it was clear her word would be the last, as no time was left. She said, "You were wrong in what you said this evening about the following matters"—and here she stated factual and interpretive errors he had made. And then she said, "Only fools underestimate me. I hoped you would not be one of them."

She exposed not only the prince's ugly ambitions but also his strategic stupidity in miscalculating the true power at the table. And knowing something about the heart of cowardice, how it loves being dominated, she created a bond of respect between herself and the prince. It excited him to be exposed for what he was: a fool, a child who needed a spanking. The woman and the feckless prince might never be compatriots, but never again would a worm like him think he could overcome her without cost to himself.

Hate and wait, and meantime weave a shroud.

Stop thinking like a woman and start thinking like your foes.

Like the sex drive—Libido—there is a death drive called Destrudo: the excitement brought on by destructiveness. Call down your wrath: realize that not everything has meaning. Don't look for meaning or try to supply it. Instead, invite in the forces of chaos. Destruction can be a worthwhile reaction. The Great Mother in her heightened femininity is as much a Destroyer as a Creator. Some people in this world are evil, or are evil at some time. No explanation suffices. To try to find one paralyzes you from acting.

The princessa was advised to follow the Five Whys: to ask why someone had committed an act meant to hurt her for what seemed no reason. She was then to ask why again and again—five times—each time boring deeper into her antagonist's motives, so she might understand and thus appeal to the better angel of his nature. But with age, *why* means less and less. One hasn't the time or patience for one, much less five, Whys. Motives are irrelevant. A loving deed is loving, a nasty deed is nasty. End of story.

You will despair of this tactic. It will seem impossible that criticism against you has no meaning or is in some way uninvited. But bilious treatment is the viper of unconscious rage in search of a target. Some attackers humiliate with words they do not mean;

they fire buckshot to distract and weaken. They may say "I just didn't feel anything" after lovemaking or demean some quality in a politician, as when Hillary Clinton was personally attacked by a journalist who called her "Saint Hillary" because she expressed concern for the soul of America in the early 1990s. "Saint Hillary" became a weapon in the hands of her critics to make Mrs. Clinton seem unwarrantedly ridiculous. Such attacks must be treated the same way: as a threat that is nevertheless utterly meaningless in content.

Put yourself in a position of ultimate authority. Administer dose after dose of humiliation. Do not respond to the charges against you. Tell the source of attacks that he is a scoundrel, a bore, a demon. Make him wonder what you mean. Do not say, "I understand you..." Attack him again and again. Repetition will give you a sense of control. A baby throws her doll out of the crib a hundred times and her parent replaces it; repetition is primal succor: it makes you feel in control of your world.

If the critic comes back heaping blame against you: "You were the one who [fill in the blank with any charge against you] twisted the knife in *my* heart," or "You always second-guessed me." Such critics do not accept the fact that their brutality caused your anger; be sure they will never understand their culpability. Ignore an antagonist's halfhearted attempts at making you think he understands anything about the emotional landscape of your dispute. These are his ruses. Make him suffer and you have at least a chance of waking him up to his responsibility.

Weave dark shrouds: indulge in meaninglessness.

Refuse to explain yourself—that is the height of tough and seasoned comic heroism. This forces others to look inward, rather than to you, for a revelation or reason. This is stronger than direct control. This is how the Entangling Woman entangles: equivocations and ambiguities, even riddles like the Sphinx's keep others off their footing. These are a form of dark flirtation. If you try to reason with malice, you have lost the battle before it began.

A woman wrote to a former lover who was trying to set her friends against her, "Oh yes, you still know exactly what is in half of my heart." Well, this means nothing and so it is funny. Her antagonist spent a fair amount of time trying to figure out what she meant before calling her bluff. But she went on with communications that deliberately veered between clear, less hazy, and downright confusing.

Say, "Oh, X, I love your playfulness and wit." Flatter your foe with the very things you admire/d about him, but each time he reaches out for clarification, respond with another quippy and affectionate non sequitur. He will become increasingly so perplexed that he will actually begin treating you sanely and yearning for your comfort.

Keep your attacks and communications in the passive voice: to phrase something like, "The things worth thinking about here are . . ." It will sound impersonal of course, but also "voiceless" and destabilizing. The passive voice makes it harder for the other to attack you, as if you move in camouflage.

Above all, assume control.

Use his name frequently. "Listen to this [pause for a beat], Conrad . . ." "How would you handle this, Conrad?" Stating the person's name followed by a pause, captivates.

Allow your eyes to sweep his. As you speak, look into his eyes. Move your glance from his left eye to his right eye with every beat of your sentence. If you are saying, "We need to talk about your dreadful behavior last night to see what we might do to fix it," you will instinctively feel the sentence broken up into beats or pauses: "We need to talk / about your dreadful behavior last night / and to see / what we might do / to fix it." With each beat, shift your eyes from his left eye to right eye. This grabs your listener's attention and puts him into a trance. He cannot escape the movement of your eyes back and forth. His eyes are locked upon yours. It is trance-inducing. At an unconscious level, it limits a listener's resistance to what you are saying.

The same effect may be created when you sit opposite someone with your muscles contracted: an isometric look. Muscles contracted project energy, vitality, animation: hard to resist.

Next, don't hold anything back: singe the king of Spain's beard.

The supreme prodigy of maturity is to be more angry, not less. To be angry about the wrongs you have suffered and about the state of the world. Female politicians cannot be angry enough. It is a sign of their honesty and their commitment to repair as only women are thought able to do.

In 1587, when she was fifty-five years old and had been on the throne for thirty years, Elizabeth I, the queen who contra Machiavelli ruled more by love than by fear, went on the offensive, a new habit in the course of her reign. She was thrown off her game, which was to continue to abide peacefully with her neighbors. It was the basis for her immense popularity: thirty years of England's peace while half of Europe was in flames meant light taxation and growing wealth and population. Like Edith Wharton shocked by Fullerton's betrayals, Elizabeth I was shocked by the appearance of King Philip's Spanish fleet in England's waters. From a persistent conviction that Philip could be brought to reason, she first had to defend herself—and her country—and then go on the offensive. There were two offensive strategies: to attack Spain from a distance, striking at the Spanish Indies. Or to singe the king of Spain's beard by attacking his treasured fleet in open waters, so close to him so that he would burn.

So she launched her attack. Singeing the king's beard meant taking action against assault (invasion) before the opposing fleet could set sail.

Going on the offensive is a common old-lady maneuver, and a change from youth . . . which depends on reaction / resistance.

Take emotion out and triumph . . . to be disentangled from extreme situations is to be emotionless . . .

If you feel emotion, go with its exact opposite.

Emotions will hold you back from what must be done. You will fight clean of all baggage if you dispose of sentiment. To be "without emotion" is terra incognita for most women, which is why it is so intoxicating.

If you feel sympathy for a nasty idiot, then lay on the contempt. If he sounds sincere, swipe him with "My dearest, you're such a phony." Soon you get to the point where he breaks his hold or you earn his respect.

Deprive him of everything and he'll give you anything.

Ignore him and you will receive ten more outbursts including self-pitying sobs, pleas of illness, and requests for pardons. Foes who appear to relent are emotional con artists. Once they have your empathy, they have won. Send a message calling attention to what you are doing: "I have no intention of replying to your sad, self-pitying messages," which of course is a reply, purposely.

Be pungently revolting to him and let him know he has finally met his superior.

Anger is like pepper on a salad. Use it. Show you are ready, willing, and able to keep the bilious exchange alive. Either he will rise to the bait and recognize that it *is* a challenge: the attack will become a kind of Tracy/ Hepburn game that you might enjoy and might shift your bond from hatred to admiration. Or he will detach from the game entirely and find a new victim or find the awful game has left him spent.

It takes a real power for a woman to shift her expectations from logical consequences in which closure plays a part to something more like a desire for continuation, neither for a happy ending or for a final solution but for freedom.

Dismiss all hope of resolution. Closure is
not *Winning.*

Hate and wait is a new style of storytelling. A new voice
of narrative power to shape events and avoid meaning.
Meaning, we shall see, is not always meaningful.

Women have lived too much with closure. The comfort of something being over, settled, and contented is
the delusion of a passive life—and the hate-and-wait
royals are not passive. "When the hope for closure is
abandoned, when there is an end to fantasy, adventure
for women will begin. Endings are for romance novels
or daydreams, but not for life."

Closure is important only if we feel that the greatest power we have is the power of saying *no.* Closure
appears so satisfying because it is the enemy of doubt:
marry him or leave him. Doubt is very laming to the
young but in later life it is the beginning of wisdom.
Doubt is a condition of openness.

The opposite of closure is disclosure, or discovery.
When you are not enclosed by closure, you will feel
both autonomous and linked, free and grounded, trea-
suring solitude and the vitality of an open life—which
may include a devoted partner and many admirers and
detractors.

Those who arrive at maturity do not make new life;
they rearrange what is already at hand.

Sidestep the need for narrative closure, which you do every time you, in your words and behavior, rewrite the story of loss as pain into the story of purity, pleasure, and play.

Tell your critics, "You can say anything to me. A blow from you will always be a caress." Once you have demonstrated your strength, a blow will be a caress: they cannot hurt or constrain you.

To rearrange what is at hand, not hurry it to an end, brings to the surface a truth hidden from sight. Laughing at the devils of Time works. Be experimental; that is the privilege of surviving. Experiments strengthen the experimenter.

And now we may restore our Mona Lisa, our magic mirror, to her perch, admired and admiring those who assemble before her.

Permit people moments of
privileged madness. Permit them to
feel their anger and sorrow—and to
forget for a time so-called sweet reason. The
voice of female gravitas doesn't want
us to reason, but to see anew.

One attribute in particular distinguishes princes and princessas from kings and queens and separates even the seasoned leader from the truly elect: that is the jewel-tone of respect that in antiques and art is called patina. In humans it is called gravitas and marks the visibility of the soul upon the flesh. It suggests the character of a long history and a long future. The Mona Lisa was painted to look instantly time-honored beneath layers of dusky lacquer. The grime of years has further darkened her face. If she were to be completely covered in soot, it is believed that crowds would still gather obsessively around her and peer in even more intently than ever for whatever traces of the old face might still be gleaned.

Gravitas is the visibility of age on a human masterpiece. It suggests a person has achieved an artful artlessness—the natural *sprezzatura* of the born aristocrat with few constraints upon her: the ability to act, think, and talk without effort: the difference between smart and serious, loyal and noble, reliable and priestly.

Gravitas is a different quality for men than for women. For men, it is eloquence in silence and a presence full of either menace or Zen, weight or weightlessness—packaged as the sweeping statement. Women may become brilliant comediennes, glorious teachers, even irresistible haters. But they do not acquire gravitas by any of these means or by means of making sweeping statements. Men hold forth on "the road to reality" or "the reason for war." They release into the air regular and thunderous eruptions about the state of the universe, or the soul, or the environment. Sweeping statements, objective assessments, heroic opinions are not the coin by which women pass into the rarest inner circles of power. A woman may speak about serious matters, and in the halls of power she sounds like Oprah, who is great indeed, but is not received with the same immortal force as Schopenhauer or Bill Gates.

Yet gravitas is vital. There may be women nominated for a nation's presidency or summoned for board

chairmanships or considered for orchestra conductor-
ships who lack gravitas. But only a woman *with* gravitas will succeed in being chosen.

Simply having an audience does not do it. An important female anchor with millions of fans may still be dismissed as lightweight. Nor does a loud or powerful voice
do it. One of the loudest voices, the journalist Oriana
Fallaci's, proved as unenlightening as a nail hammered
into a thumb: "You've got to get old, because you have
nothing to lose. You have this respectability that is given
to you, more or less. But you don't give a damn. It is the
ne plus ultra of freedom. And things that I didn't used to
say before—you know, there is in each of us a form of
timidity, of cautiousness—now I open my big mouth. I
say, 'What the f*** are you going to do to me?'…I say
what I want." Though what she said was right, the cater-
wauling style cost her the aristo coin of gravitas.

For every twenty comedic heroines, there is one mature voice that masters the sweeping statement with
just the right touch to get the higher authorities to pay
attention: the journalist and commentator Barbara
Ehrenreich speaks truth to power straight. She is a rar-
ity in a culture where every mongrel boy is sought for
pronouncements on the big subjects of war, politics,
economy, and the future because she takes on boy subjects—politics and the economy—from an underdog
perspective, and then she does something males do

not do: she participates in her subjects' lives. Her book *Nickel and Dimed*, which is about America's working poor, became a touchstone of public debate, a play that opened in Los Angeles, and a political movement for raising the minimum wage by law. Few women acquire that level of social seriousness; yet, in age, women wish for just such statecraft-as-soulcraft impact.

Ehrenreich is one of the few whose voice has attained respect without following the intermediate comedic heroine route. For a woman who has used the perfume of comedy to beguile others and who wants more of a direct voice in public affairs, history offers the following tactical response:

Begin with your own death.

*To make sweeping statements—the kind that hold forth about the war and the economy and all matters of the gravest concern—*one must stop being seen as a clown. The comic heroism that gave you power to a certain point must, sooner or later, end.

The mature woman must stage her own death—so to speak. The dead gain the stature to say anything. By dead we mean speaking from a story of loss—of a person, or one's position, or a perceived loss of social standing. Jackie Kennedy told the journalist William Manchester that no one would believe anything bad about her because of the suffering she had endured. Soon after the Monica Lewinsky scandal became headline news, Hillary Clinton, still in the death grip of shame, received a standing ovation by simply walking onto the stage of the prestigious and largely male membership of the World Economic Forum in Davos. Wearing the ashes of an old life is also suitable, as if you had come back from death itself, like Inanna. A conversion too is a kind of death; when you give up some old point of view and acquire another, you become someone else. Make these deaths part of your story, part of your public identity, and you gain gravitas.

A death may also be a withdrawal from public life. The Texas senator Barbara Jordan left the Senate at age forty-five and found "a new sense of her own power." She called her youth "my other life...[when] I was in the spiral to get ahead....I was forty years old before I decided I really could turn my head and look in another direction."

By making much of your losses, you become an aristocrat. The thing most people wait for—a loss that you have faced or a terrible fear—you have experienced. You already have your trauma, and this sets you apart.

Loss becomes your message, which sets you apart from men and the young who overemphasize the importance of winners.

The last words of the philosopher Hannah Arendt, found in her typewriter the day she died, were from Cato the Elder: "The winning cause pleased the gods, but the losing cause pleases Cato." The losing cause also pleased Arendt. She argued for expiatory circumstances regarding the terrible crimes against humanity of Adolf Eichmann, the Nazi commandant, whose trial on fifteen counts of murder she covered beginning in 1961. Her phrase, "the banality of evil," defined a new kind of political debauch. The work of a reporter was new to Arendt, then forty-five—an experiment. She took to it with freshness, vigor, and courage. There was no more losing battle than arguing that a murderer regarded as an archvillain was not evil, merely an unthinking bureaucrat following orders in an evil system, the Third Reich. Arendt established herself as a thinker whose ideas had to be reckoned with. For women, in maturity, the losing side proves the winning side.

How to Get Others to Redream Your Dream

Men's gravitas is dry-eyed and distant, noble and detached: typical is the exalted vocabulary of moral or spiritual leadership. Men who are the driest sticks of timber, without any emotional valence at all, humanize but also ennoble themselves by using words like "calling," "purpose," "calmness," "character," "strength." The use of such words about another person or a situation always redounds upon the male speaker. A man who uses them is mirrored as a figure of purpose, character, strength, etcetera. He basks in the reflected glory of these words and thus gains gravitas. But a woman will only sound shallow or presumptive rather than "to the manor born" by using these heroic terms from the hoary realm of tragedy.

Rather, the voice of *female* gravitas rests upon the cusp between women's homespun or comedic roots and their extremes, which is a kind of exotic seriousness. *The voice of female gravitas is meant to release others to dionysiac, wild, and untamed impulses.* Female gravitas is meant to satisfy people's shamefaced longing (otherwise repressed or sublimated) to be driven out of control—with anger or rage. But most of all, to attain gravitas, a mature woman arouses shame.

The high priestess of gravitas, Harriet Beecher Stowe, threw caution to the winds and boldly took a position on freedom and justice—the losing side that she turned into the winning side. Her statements, rendered in a novel called *Uncle Tom's Cabin*, published in serial form during 1851 and 1852, are a pivotal lesson in how a mature feminine voice achieves gravitas.

To speak truth to power directly, begin recounting suffering or pain. But go further; go for the jugular. Arouse others with liberal doses of blatant sentiment. Grave women convey statements that are full of ecstatic feeling. Feeling that isn't drily presented but that takes possession of others, as if in a prophetic voice. The junior senator from Texas Barbara Jordan opened her speech for Richard Nixon's impeachment by reminding listeners that the Constitution's phrase "We the people" did not for more than one hundred years mean her—a woman of color. She expressed her loss in a rational argument about constitutional law; her passion was all the more intense and arousing because she was speaking about her loss. Jordan gave this speech as an unknown legislator on the Senate floor at 2 a.m. She should have been ignored. Instead she made headlines and won a national platform for her ideas. The sentiment she evokes of white guilt for blacks is rousing to this day.

Women may not merely voice opinions, if they wish to be heard. Rather they must spin epics arousing shame in a completely different voice from men or the young. It is the means by which a woman may slip through the fourth wall of Time, slowing strangers down to listen to her, to attend the urgency in women's voices. Mrs. Stowe wrote not merely the great American novel but the greatest American novel ever—if considered as a work that, like the Declaration of Independence and the Constitution, changed a nation. Yet few read her today in schools. She made no case for personal toughness as did Hemingway, Mark Twain, or any of the so-called American masters whose works dominate school curricula. Mrs. Stowe merely altered a nation's destiny.

Her message: Bear witness to shame.

President Abraham Lincoln called Mrs. Stowe "the little woman who started the great war." She did what not even Lincoln could do. *Uncle Tom's Cabin* was read by millions in tears, terror, outrage, and guilt for what she drew in epic terms about slavery. She roused support to start a war to end slavery. She changed people's minds. That is gravitas.

Women's voices may change women's lives; but almost never do female voices remap heaven and earth. Mrs. Stowe changed the terms of engagement, however, and she did it in a female voice. Mrs. Stowe made her statements on behalf of others, but also spoke for herself. She was facing many insecurities when she wrote *Uncle Tom's Cabin*. These insecurities were her fear of growing old, her conviction that she was not beautiful, her inability to control or protect her children (a favorite son would become an alcoholic and drift from sight), and the failure of her voice to be heard even inside her family and then too among people who had to pay attention to what she had witnessed. The racial shame she spoke was one in which people could read their own fears, as she voiced her own.

Mrs. Stowe was shameless, which made her the person to speak a nation's shame. She manipulated listeners, and they needed manipulating. Her means to bring the masses to attention was to take on a major subject—slavery, injustice—and ground her stories and her views in sentiment. Sentimental characters, extreme incidents, stories designed to provoke tears and outrage:

all the things men seek to avoid, she indulged in. Mrs. Stowe wept over the death of her baby son as if she were a slave herself—permitted few opinions in a patriarchal culture and arguing with a patriarchal God who, like the most arrogant of slave masters, tore children from the arms of their mothers or sent them into war. But *rather than personalize her experience, she unselfed herself.* She characterized her wounds as the nation's.

She was shameless in arousing tears not in calm reflection (as Aristotle requires of pure tragedy, where distance is said to increase the force of the story), but in pity and in disgust, recounting episodes of extreme situations where rape and violence but also love and forgiveness came to the forefront.

To convince people to *redream your own dreams*, a woman must speak of the cause, and only obliquely of herself. Inner and outer forces merge when she develops a "non-negotiable set of principles." If we are whole and mature, there are some very old words that will be used to define us, words like truth, virtue, honesty. Our political and policy decisions will reflect them once we are old.

But more than merely say these words, a woman must evoke them, drench people in the feeling of them. Barbara Jordan made listeners believe that Winston Churchill had been reincarnated as a black Texas woman. What awed people "was Jordan's ferocious in-

sistence that justice wasn't only for the rich and powerful." As she got older, Jordan's oratory, like that of
the Sophists of fifth-century Greece who invented the
rules of rhetoric, was more than a mere opportunity
for dramatic performance. It was a means of organiz-
ing evidence and proofs in order *to communicate truth, to
put others inside the crisis.* When she delivered her most
eloquent speeches, her audiences felt they did indeed
hear the essence of truth, not from on high *but from
in their midst.* By force of her sentiment, listeners were
uplifted, perhaps transformed momentarily into better
versions of themselves, and just as often pummeled
into realizing how insufficient they were too.

*The voice of female gravitas doesn't want us to reason,
but to see anew.* If such a voice makes people cry, it is all
to the good as the masculine ideal that art, ideas, agendas have to be distanced, detached, and controlled is
punctured by the force of women's public voices. This
voice's arousal to action is a tremendous act of grace.

Female gravitas will not appeal to or persuade the
elite, not the *New York Times* or the *New Yorker* or the *New
Republic* crowd. It will be dismissed as inelegant. But it
will stir public response outside centers of power and ultimately incur respect inside them. Sentiment and ecstasy
always break through the barricades of reason.

Mrs. Stowe's inelegant subjects were sex and violence together with love and forgiveness ... Everything

was couched in these tones: and it wrung tears from people's eyes. People wish to be brought to tears and understand—to connect to—human suffering. She called for sacrifice from Americans and they gave it with their lives, by the millions.

Women often ask a priestly woman, "What is it about you that commands people to attention?" The answer is always, "They are led by the all too human desire to be released to sentiment and sacrifice."

No one is spared in Mrs. Stowe's or Hannah Arendt's minds: we come to see how all are implicated in a woman's analyses of injustice; there are no bad guys and good guys in such tales. People share in the blame.

Female gravitas is the voice not of the tough, wandering hero but of the person who is sitting very still and attending to what is going on in her own home, of finding the grandeur in shame.

Anyone who wishes to enter the Kingdom of the Mothers knows that a sacrifice is possible and necessary. It is the essential female myth, that every living person must sacrifice him or herself ultimately to Mother Earth. One must eventually return to dust. The sacrifice for which the Mothers—and Mrs. Stowe is a human version of this—call is for listeners to be released from the trap of their own limits. To experience Cleopatra's vivacity, for example, the Roman general Antony knew he must surrender to her, not only love her. He must surrender his insistent masculinity for the pleasures of the feminine world as against policing Caesar's empire. Nathaniel Branden, allying himself with Ayn Rand, was told directly that their relationship would be sexual or nothing at all—requiring he sacrifice his brand-new marriage. Mrs. Stowe required sacrifice to prove Americans better in judgment and habit and thus lessen a nation's shame. To insist upon sacrifice establishes a new vision and a woman's gravitas.

Mrs. Stowe does something else that masters of female gravitas do: she takes us into the headquarters of female power. She evokes images of spaces that are intrinsically female. For example, she reminds us that the slave quarters are Mother Africa. Cleopatra too created of her palace in Egypt a sensual place that was the opposite of Rome with its laws and seriousness.

The voice may be raging and exotic, but the setting evoked must be humble. Female gravitas evokes many images of domestic spaces wherein sacrifice is born.

We do not realize how much time people spend in these places routinely. We curl up in these rooms every night before our television sets: rooms in which sitcoms and TV dramas take place, which almost never take us outside themselves. In these rooms men and women argue, crack jokes, and confront their shame, whether the subject is love or family life or fear of the unknown. If the daylight world is devoted to politics, the world of nightly television is one big house of many rooms. It is an act of female gravitas to show that politics is framed by what happens here, and to remind all who attend that mothers and fathers are also seekers and protectors. Whatever one's topic, whatever the argument, whatever the position, revealing what happens in these rooms gives weight to one's ideas or point of view. By focusing on female reactions of sympathy and ecstasy, by evoking what happens in homes and implying the bigger picture, one invites others into the Kingdom of the Mothers.

The dionysiac release from shame: this is meant to get people to respond to your message not as observation or even storytelling, but as myth.

Mrs. Stowe makes clear what she appeals to is the domestic heart within everyone: the desire of men and women for the snowy white tablecloths, for the chambers of love and sex, for closeness, and for a clear success for the losing cause, whatever that may be, and it is usually freedom.

Cleopatra too sought to open the Kingdom of the Mothers to others, particularly her lover Antony, offering him an alternative world to the police state of the Roman Empire, offering him a release in Sentiment and Sacrifice:

> No more, but e'en a woman, and commanded
> By such poor passion as the maid that milks,
> And does the meanest chares. It were for me
> To throw my scepter at the injurious gods,
> To tell them that this world did equal theirs,
> Till they had stol'n our jewel. All's but naught:
> Patience is sottish, and impatience does
> Become a dog that's mad: then it is a sin,
> To rush into the secret house of death,
> Ere death dare come to us? How do you, women?
> What, what good cheer! Why, how now, Charmian?
> My noble girls! Ah, women, women! Look,
> Our lamp is spent, it's out. Good sirs, take heart,
> We'll bury him: and then, what's brave, what's noble,
> Let's do it after the high Roman fashion,
> And make death proud to take us. Come, away,
> This case of that huge spirit now is cold.
> Ah women, women! Come, we have no friend
> But resolution, and the briefest end.

Cleopatra refers to herself as "a woman"—as one of her kind, and very discreetly. Her words are an indoctrination to extremes, to the Kingdom of the Mothers, where patience and impatience, chores to gods, and the urgency are life and death, as all the great women's lessons are, "like the biofissure of women, cleaving between life and death." Her maids, Iras and Charmian, are moved by her speech. But she does something we all must do: *she moves herself so extraordinarily* that the effect itself becomes an added aesthetic grace.

Though the reach of female gravitas is epic and deals with the largest human problems, and although the tone is wildly Dionysiac, the language is humble, *so plain it is like prayer,* as if you are asking for something in a conversation with the largest possible interlocutor: as if everything was being addressed to God. A feeling that the world is listening to you makes you both big and small. It "unselfs the self."

Mrs. Stowe said *Uncle Tom* was written by God. Only later in life, when she tried to write anything in sweeping statements, taking on the posture of male gravitas, did she fail miserably and become a pompous scold.

To move oneself is a matter of believing in the losing cause, feeling unembarrassed by sentimentality, and one more thing: *to live as if one's entire life is about legacy—your presence in your absence.*

Be totally unself-conscious about your legacy but immersed in ideals of creating greatness out of small acts of stewardship and a sense of being part of a continuum of people entrusted to do more. The means to legacy, to living out one's destiny, are not a matter of wealth or position. To stir people to beautiful action, to do great things humbly and humble work sublimely—to make a difference are to know that you are doing such things all the time, with no certainty as to which acts will turn out to make a lasting contribution. That simply means living your life with faith that the ripple effect of even the most mundane things will be a force for good. A woman may hear (often years later) that some long-forgotten thing she did made a difference to someone.

Understand how much of an impact you have already had. Then you will be able to grab hold of the future. How exciting the future will be once you are free of negative influences.

To feel removed from history, to lack a sense of one's history, is crippling. It diminishes everything one does and makes life so transient.

Women above all should hold a sense of dynasty and place in time—how else can they fulfill a role as mothers, sisters, lovers, and beloveds? Without a sense of history all their nurturing occurs at the most basic levels, and they cannot pass on things that lead to grandeur. Women in the past—the storytellers in particular—have always had a sense of history, of continuity. How did we lose that?

Feed the flame of your charisma,
because all who stand before you
wish to enter your circle.

Men who have late-life crises buy cars, women build organizations—for the same reasons. Both want the thrill, the speed, the head-turning pleasure of getting where they want to go *elegantly*.

The form the mature favor is the circle. Like Lamborghinis, circles allow one to round corners fast and tight with zero degrees of separation between people inside them. In a circle, one is instantly connected to others one wishes to reach. The kind of circle mature women favor is the court.

The model is Leonardo's woman. All who stand before the Mona Lisa enter her circle. The painting creates a bubble around itself; many who are drawn to her do not emerge again, not for their whole lives. They forever remember seeing her and what it did to them. A woman may create structures that encircle others with her purpose, presence, and gravitas.

Nothing is sexier than a woman who sits at the center of a court, encircled by appreciation—not banished to the top of some organizational ladder, lonely and alone. There are no glass ceilings in maturity. Perhaps there never were any; only the insufficiencies or blindness of youth made us believe there were.

Let us see how such courts are brought to life.

When youth and beauty failed women in seventeenth-century France, when marriages and other institutional rewards did not satisfy them, they relied upon moral courage to make history in their image. They created salons of talk and friendship, gatherings of passionate but not sexual love, in which ideas of freedom and revolution rivaled those of Periclean Athens—and changed the world. From dining room to dining room, the walls of each outfitted in dark red or blue damask silks and curtains, the woman at the center kept changing, but the circle stayed the same. These beautiful courts enlivened and democratized the world more completely than any routine form of organization.

Why endure boredom when one is at war with Time? As George Eliot said, "Women have short strings for monotony and so develop an instinctive lightness of treatment which makes them reject all heaviness."

Women do not fancy a "Built to Last" belief that the best organizations are those that are around forever. In truth, lasting organizations are of the same species as cockroaches and dinosaurs: witless, mechanical, and dully unattractive—same old, same old. They may change their form, but their sodden spirit persists. Such organizations are rarely homes for women's goals or spirit.

Much more interesting are the missions and groups that form collaboratively to experiment with new ideas. Of course, there is Julia's kitchen which created a fellowship around cooking, and Chanel's atelier. Beyond these iconic figures are Katharine White, who became the valued editor at the *New Yorker*—her writers her thriving circle; Barbara Epstein was similarly the heartbeat of the profitable and influential periodical the *New York Review of Books*; she inspired in her writers and colleagues a feeling of being enveloped by her brilliance and wit; Edith Wharton's reading room invited in other writers to converse about books. These are not dreary organizations bent on self-preservation first and foremost but circles of enlivening practices.

Courts make room for the most unlikely fellow travelers and turn them into kin, not just colleagues. Circles are not all built to last but to be gorgeously indifferent to Time: to form, to shimmer with influence, and then to disperse and let new connections form.

Like soap bubbles, even when they leave, they linger in the mind. Circles offer a different experience of Time. They are a matrix, not an arrow, a rest stop, not a springboard to endless progress, whatever that is. Like stories, circles last only as long as needed. Then they are retold or remade.

Of course, some of these circles do last, particularly if one of them sends out satellites, such as Saunders's St. Christopher's, which has become the model for hospice care the world over; or if it merges with a major institution, as Chanel's brand name has grown way beyond the founder's dreams.

Circles do not stultify the soul as rigid organizations do; they don't grind down people's edges, as do families and companies. Instead of imprisonment in a concentration of walls and boundaries, a circle invites lingering. Architects use circles rather than squares to break compression, to expand, and to leave no room for fatigue or habit. Circular forms respond to adjustments in consciousness that have already taken place and also set new precedents. They convince you and others that intuition can be more rigorous than reason. They are places safe as laps and voluptuous as labyrinths.

Feeding the Flame

The way queens ordered fleets into the seas and countrymen into new lands to extend their empire, we may now consider how to manage and spread influence beyond the time and space one iconic image may touch, or one voice may reach.

Only queens had the authority and resources to live as women do now with the freedom to create their own milieu. In France in the year 1170, the mind of a woman passed like an electric current through the culture, making large and imaginative what elsewhere was heavy and snooty. That mind belonged to Eleanor of Aquitaine, who redefined the circle of power.

Historians attest that there has never been a culture dominated by women. They insist that matriarchies exist only in myth and legend. But they are wrong. Matriarchies exist where they leave no shards: *in the mind and the heart*.

Eleanor's late-style power was bold by any definition. She rejected the typical form of power branded by her mother-in-law, *maîtresse femme* (master female) Matilda the Empress, who inculcated in her son the prince habits of statecraft like the "hungry falcon strategy": give people a taste of the prize but no more. Great expectations should be constantly withdrawn. "Trust only those who have a hunger based on a failing, some intrinsic element of the soul that makes them unable to be fulfilled by what they acquire and therefore always need more."

Eleanor married Matilda's son, King Henry II of

England. Once her independence caught up to her anger, loss, and comic touch, she took this hideous philosophy and turned the nasty elements into the one thing everyone hungers for and wants more and more of: love. In Eleanor's planning, shared power became something mythic, a new creation: the court of love...*a place where destruction of illusion holds a power equal to creation*...Such places are said to be allied to the devil and destruction, but they are really allied to nature, which is creativity, the greatest power.

Eleanor fled from Henry, her power-hungry husband, whom she loved but who had fallen under the spell of a young mistress. At age forty-eight, she returned to her own city of Poitiers with her children, rejecting the imperfect destiny to which she had been, it seemed, assigned. She would be no one's pawn. She was, as such queens tend to be, intense and rapid rather than comprehensive. Such women produce crystallizations of great ideas that float through their minds; they seem able to create a spell that will arrest these ideas, giving them prominence for others to see.

In her princessa years, Eleanor had ridden beside her first husband, Louis VII, on the Crusade to Jerusalem—a feat in itself, but to spark the troops on the difficult journey, she rode bare-breasted. After the humbling at Henry's hands, she would create another world, as feminine as the one of her youth but larger and more shockingly naked, in a way.

She built a territory in Poitiers dedicated not to war, religion, or any king, but to women (Minerva, Venus, and the Virgin). She created a court of love. With it she made her three declarations of power, necessary conditions for a woman to draw a circle around her; as historian Amy Kelly notes:

- to escape from secondary roles as wife and helper
- to assert her independent sovereignty
- to dispense her own justice and her own patronage

To bring order to the court, Eleanor expanded on the arts of love from the classical form in which man is the master and seducer to a philosophy in which woman is the mistress, man her pupil in homage, her vassal in service.

Eleanor's upside-down court was like the petals that the wind shakes from the rose in its bloom: an idea borne of strife and uncramped by timidity. It overturned the rules and created a golden world. A woman's right was to draw men from the hunt and from dice to games of feminine society. Boorishness was outlawed and adulations of women compelled. The courts ruled on lovers' complaints, like one brought by a knight who believed himself too harshly judged by his lover. Eleanor believed that true love could not exist between a husband and wife. Her judgment: "Mortal love is but the licking of honey from thorns." After these sessions, political matters were discussed. Eleanor believed the court was more clear-sighted discussing war only after adjudicating matters of love.

The court attracted the younger generation, while the old guard clustered around Henry. A dozen royal children, her own and cousins, joined Eleanor. Her household became a nursery and academy of prospective Olympians—kings and queens, dukes and princesses.

Her court inevitably became a competitor to Henry's. When Henry offered to take Eleanor back and end her experiment, she ignored him. In return, he committed acts of terror close to her capital, setting fires and thieving. Disguised in men's clothes, she tried to escape but was caught. Henry had her jailed. He could divorce her, but Eleanor would, he knew, easily make allies to oppose him. At fifty-three, divorced, she could be sent to a nunnery. She refused to renounce her inheritance of lands—Poitiers—so Henry locked her up.

She was his strategic match, and their plays of war and oddly love, too, intrigued him and tested him as no one and nothing else could. Her survival became, to her, a mental chess game, and so even a bad fate turned comic.

Except for holidays with Henry and her sons, Eleanor remained imprisoned for fifteen years and was released at age sixty-eight upon Henry's death. Release from prison was a rebirth. She guided her son Richard, the new king, in reversing Henry's policies.

No king in Europe had more experience with men and affairs than she. Eleanor had survived two husbands and had had two sons crowned king. Love, courtliness, and gallantry persist in human affairs because of poets' faith in them and because of the rituals of romance that the court of Eleanor created. Love brought people to the court, and freed them to leave as necessary. Eleanor's idea of love lives in people's minds to this day. This is the value of circles created by women: even when they end, they continue in the mind.

All successful circles obey this rule:

Matriarchies are arguments with society as a whole.

Eleanor of Aquitaine created the court of love to oppose and balance her husband's court. Like all matriarchal forms, it is blatantly anti-elephant: the opposite of old, big, and slow. It is the habit of maturity to go against the things of current time in favor of the Timeless.

Courts may also be so individualistic and intimate that they exist best in the imagination: the poet Emily Dickinson's circle was very small, limited to close family and a few chosen acquaintances. She lived a private existence, with no coteries, almost no sustaining professional gossip. Her coping methods: friendships that were like her poetry, creations of her imagination—"worlds"—in which she could live the only kind of life possible for her. A circle must be exactly that kind of place: where one may live her own life, as defined by her. Dickinson endowed each of her friends with whatever qualities her own nature required, and regardless of reciprocity: she lived within an ambience of her own creation. She wished to link herself to people's essence, whatever it was in a new friend that would spark her imagination. Her sister-in-law, Sue, became her dearest woman friend, Thomas Higginson her literary link to the public world, Judge Lord her hope for marriage—such a tiny circle, each member more important to her when kept at a distance marked by letter or leavetaking. Essence, for her, required absence. Love comes after the guest leaves, she said, because "only then can it be disentangled from its accidents and truly known."

Be Nice to Mice

The Mona Lisa draws strangers into her world in large part because she sits between two summits, her eyes at the line of the horizon: modern paintings show fewer and fewer horizons because people are confused about where they stand. You, at the center of your court, may offer people a perspective and thus a place to stand.

As the figure in the painting lures circles of visitors, so lionesses in winter entice mice. From Colette's lair— her "mousetrap," she called her home, which drew admirers from far and wide—she regarded her admirers "with the gaze of a pensive wild animal." Her permed and hennaed hair appeared like "the tawny mane of a captive lioness." She was amused by the human spectators admitted to her cage. Once their curiosity had been satisfied, visitors didn't know what to say, the roles were reversed, and it was the lioness who threw them the tidbits of a few words.

The eye, said Emerson, *is the first circle*. You lure people in by the intensity of your attention and intention. These confer a state of grace. The people closest to you teach you what love is, and they receive the strongest light of your gaze. Hollywood moguls asked Gertrude Stein how, at age fifty-nine, she was able to attract such large crowds to her speeches—she, a writer who had a tendency not to talk down to people. Stein had been an archly playful writer, a true comedic heroine, whose work had been torturously obscure and relished only by her closest friends, until her breakthrough work, *The Autobiography of Alice B. Toklas*, appeared in 1933. She had never been one to pander to the masses, and she explained her vast popularity this way: "I have a small group of friends." Those friends loved her and were grateful to her. Their friendships became so strong—the stuff of legend. They carried the message of Stein's hospitality and loyalty far and wide. To achieve a sturdy circle, one must mature a group of close friends.

A person's presence extends in a radius of roughly seven feet around her. But after you reach age fifty, that radius shrinks and continues to shrink as time goes on. Others must get closer to notice and thus to appreciate you. Or they must get close to those to whom you are close. Thus mousetrap becomes essential to building a circle.

As you get good at finding new people, your circle becomes the whole world. Margaret Mead—scholar, teacher, mother, and godmother of the revived discipline of anthropology—saw herself not only as her brothers' and sisters' keeper but the keeper also of her neighbors, countrymen, and in due course, her enemies. To become our enemies' keepers as well as our brothers' is something no women on earth have yet learned to be, or any men. We believe we do not have responsibility for our enemies. But once we become our enemies' keepers, a grade of evolution will be reached. What is needed, Mead said, is "the invention that will protect every member of the human species with the sanctions that once stretched no farther than a stone could be thrown." Mead stretched farther and wider and in more directions. People said of her, "Oh, she was so *large*," and it was clear they were not referring to her girth.

She stayed large by not drifting from former in-laws and distant relatives, nor from former students. She energetically sought them out, demanding to know how Time was treating them. Mead's enduring legacy, and her most endearing charm, is the bold and generous way she defined the word "family."

Gathered around the Mona Lisa are perhaps twenty people at a given moment, and then they move on to make space for another twenty, and then twenty more. They look at her as if they are staring in a mirror; they take on her slight smile and calmness. So the members of a circle mirror themselves in whomever they consider the center at any given time. We may say there are two kinds of familial likeness: one based on genes, as in families, which include many differences. The other kind of likeness is that of a flame lighting another flame: the likenesses between two flames are much greater. Members of a circle are more like candle flames.

The legendary food writer M. F. K. Fisher was abandoned by her family circle, by her daughters who felt alienated by her independent spirit, and by three husbands whom she lost to death and divorce. She acquired a new family in maturity: no dependents, only peers, culinary illuminati James Beard, Julia Child, and others in her professional world. Their interests mirrored her own. They welcomed her as an equal. Unlike her unappreciative children and unfaithful spouses, this family loved her mutually and unconditionally. For the first time she knew her potential to live a life as vast as theirs.

Mighty Motivational Mousetraps, or How the Ripe Are Kindest to the Raw

People said that a day with Eleanor of Aquitaine or Margaret Mead or M. F. K. Fisher caused them to see life more clearly than they had seen it before.

Mead was the matriarch to hundreds of students and professionals. She helped them see where they stood in the scheme of things. She was a platform builder, making a kind of maternal "lap" that welcomed many. She helped people build their own platforms and then stood upon theirs too.

A sense of oneself as an original gives a woman a strange integrity and allows her to press her image upon others. Mead was a so-so scholar and a good enough teacher. But as a matriarch, she had uncontested genius. She cultivated elements of uniqueness to excite others' interest less in her than in her work, as when she chose an ancient walking stick instead of a conventional cane when her leg gave out.

Her mousetraps were ingenious and original, each a means to build a circle:

Show Up Empty-Handed.

Poverty is a blessed beginning, Mead believed. She would enter a stranger's house or office, sit with her palms up as if to say, "I come empty-handed, I carry no weapons, I am here to receive, show me." She sat this way even though it was uncomfortable and did it especially with children. To sit this way at a gathering is at first odd but soon draws from others the most robust conversation. Mead was everybody's teacher, but everybody was hers too. When she assigned papers to her classes, she would implore them to "teach me something!" and when they obliged, she was delighted. It bound others to her; they always remembered what she taught them, but even more, what they taught her.

Gift others with pieces of the self.

Mead often sent people things she cherished and had owned for years. In recompense, when a young friend was ordained as a deacon, he sent Mead a special vestment he had worn for the ceremony. The gift forged the intimacy of their relationship. They both felt from then on that they could transcend Time and Space, that they would never be absent from each other's presence. Through such means, one begins forging bonds of thorough and explicit communication.

Demonstrate the sharp compassion of the healer's art.

Mead was ruthless when confronted, but she loved arguments. It gave people a great respect for her . . . for the degree to which she persisted in expressing her values. Her method was razor sharp. She was as much a therapist to others as a teacher who could return people to a golden time when it was safe to speak your mind.

Engage in whitemail.

Agree to help a person by offering a favor to another who can be of help to that person. To be indirect in your gifting is very purposeful: you do not appear to be currying favor with your generosity.

Seek substance in your encounters and visits.

Take stock of religious days and practice high-quality worship. Appreciate them as rituals, observing Sabbath Saturdays and Sundays, for example. It is a means for drawing others to you—to infect as many people as possible with your own passionate involvements. Mead was not in favor of religious exclusion. She wanted no part of anything that excluded her from others, as sexual and religious ecstasy tend to do. In age, the temperament has already pruned away what might be superfluous. Its new job is to rake in everything that might prove useful. She was a fisher of persons.

Never hold grudges against other women.

Mead drew together lots of young women as her researchers, teaching assistants, and in all kinds of ad hoc sororities. She believed that women's relationships with women should be conciliatory to a fault. Mead made a "serious new friend" every two or three months and added the new name immediately to her Christmas card list. We see this too in the *salonistes*, the Frenchwomen who invited men into their society and taught them freedom, civility, and the affairs of the world. Their centrality to the important people they cultivated made them "persons through whose hands the secrets of the whole world had to pass," wrote one of them, Madame d'Orleans. The women made themselves valuable and trusted friends of women and men, who demonstrated whenever possible large capacity and large heart.

Mother in two directions.

Mead taught and mothered young women, even as they mothered her, buying her queen-size panty hose, massaging her back when she fell ill, picking up her dry cleaning, and keeping her stocked with Dexedrine. As one said, "If she'd been a man, I'd have had grounds for a lawsuit." Colleagues felt they were more than sisters; they were her great friends. And men became her long-lost brothers. It was said of the French *salonistes* that, whether or not they were geniuses, they were women whom men could love and who could make women their friend, confidante, and counselor, the sharer not of their joys and sorrows only, but of their ideas and aims.

Provide a crossing to safety.

Matriarchal circles provide for marriages of minds, and if we wish to elicit the truth and beauty of life, we must draw people by providing them a sense of well-being, not a retreat from reality. Safe places are not refuges from anyplace. They are restorations of a golden time. People are not attracted to places that are free of disagreement; rather, more discussion occurs in places that make them feel safe and that introduce provocation. Institutionalized salons—conferences— evoke this when they are hosted by universities rather than staged in hotels. Collaborations offer the same safety-to-provocation ratio as salons. Projects on which to work together for pleasure or play instead of a clear end also make it possible for people to be safe again as in childhood and thus fully alive.

Know that much happiness depends on people's experience of the ends of things.

Mead liked rituals that marked the end of things. Everyone marks the start of something, but ends have a certain nostalgia and supportiveness that go beyond celebrating the birth of a baby or a wedding. When a household disbanded, she believed the event should be marked by a party: a housecooling. She felt the same would be useful for divorcing couples, so the divorced feel part of a community. She sought to create places where judgment is suspended and where values can be tested, in thought and speech.

Cool kisses ignite the longest flame.

Mead would often kiss a friend in a way that was not maternal but more effusive and warm, allowing them to see the soft side of that fierce professionalism.

What's good for the beehive is good for the bee.

A supplicant for whom Mead offered to give a free public lecture told her he didn't want to use her or take advantage of her. "You can only use a person," she answered, "when you're taking something from them that can't be replaced. There is nothing I wouldn't do for you." For those in your circle, there should be nothing you would not do. Giving energy replenishes energy.

A Woman at the Center of a Circle Needs Two Homes: One in Which She Lives and One in Which She Really Lives

Of the two homes women need, the second, said Gertrude Stein, "is her fantasy home."

The fantasy home may be real but with elements of the unreal: "Will you come to the world of my dreams if I manage to find my way there?" George Sand asks, inviting her young admirer, Gustave Flaubert, to visit Nohant, her spiritual center. Nohant was off center, a country home that was her court of love, her stand against Parisian politics and professional skirmishes. At Nohant she wrote books and gathered family and lovers into safety around her.

A fantasy home changes reality. In the days after she left the White House, the newly widowed, the matured Jackie Kennedy set herself up in a new home. It was a town house loaned to her. But she could be said to inhabit more fully her second home—a fantasy home of her own creation or reinvention: the court of Camelot. Jackie constructed the myth that her husband's presidency was the realization of heroic legend, a presidency too pure in its goals of democracy, equality, and the arts to last even a full presidential term. By this one stroke of imaginative vision, she gave Kennedy's brief and flawed administration a quality beyond Time, and eternal nobility. The legendary Camelot was marked by the Round Table, where justice and love prevailed. The Camelot presidency colors history perhaps even more thoroughly than the real historical record of her husband's presidency. Circles trump logical squares, particularly over Time and in the imagination.

Julia Child's kitchen was as much Julia's second home as a turtle's shell is both house and owner's skin. The idea of it, the legend it inspires, continues on after her death. It grew into a second or fantasy home. At first Julia's place was a small circle—herself and two collaborators working on a serious book that most publishers thought had no audience. *Mastery of French Cooking* was an unwieldy manuscript rejected by Houghton when Julia was a year shy of fifty.

This is one of the hallmarks of mature leadership: Child went against her time; she was deliberately anachronistic—not caring if she had readers, as one has a baby based on pure faith that the future will provide, without knowing what the child's eventual place in the world will be. The book, a bible on French cooking at a time when Velveeta dominated the gourmet section of grocery stores, seemed an improbable bet. A cookbook had never before sparked a social revolution. But this one did: the household arts became artistry and women became professionals at cooking. Julia's legacy is linked to circles upon circles whose members endlessly pay her homage to this day. Child made a platform for herself—and for the wonders of French cooking—by creating multiple platforms: teaching (via television and books), hiring dozens of apprentices and welcoming them like family, and watching them create circles of their own. She created her own second—or fantasy—home on the property of her collaborator, Simca Beck. Like Gertrude Stein, she cultivated her small circle best. Child was incredibly ambitious not only for herself, but for the art of cooking and making the effort of cooking a pleasure.

Serving the center of one's art selflessly is to draw others in to share the pleasure you feel. Julia herself was a supplicant to the art of cooking, as Mead was to the habits of people.

Centers convey a sense of abandon, an authority handed over to pleasure, whose wildest excitement comes from a form of asceticism, *not lust.*

Create a palace of genius and insanity, where, as the sculptor Louise Nevelson said, one "goes to eat caviar, drink champagne, all the things you don't do by day." Nevelson's studio—a court of the love of art—was a gathering place for young and old. The work was de-manding during the day, but at night, after the last brush was clean and all the work put away, the parties began. Discipline and joy are the bond of circles.

Pleasure carries vast authority. But it is pleasure of a

specific kind: asceticism, not lust, characterizes salons like Gertrude Stein's, schools like Madame de Maintenon's, workshops like Georgia O'Keeffe's, ateliers like Coco Chanel's couture chamber, kitchens like Julia's, and laboratories for experimentation. Each of these is defined by the fact that *the aesthetic drives the moral*—another kind of going against. Make beauty the foundational aim of your projects and, if you are consistent, your court will be lush and selfless.

A center boasts of a woman's hand.

At age sixty-one O'Keeffe gave up her New York City apartment and settled in Abiquiu, New Mexico, far from the center of the art world. Her move ended up shifting the center of the art world to include Abiquiu—as Eleanor's court shifted the center of European politics. O'Keeffe built her own matriarchate in a house made of pink walls. Workmen did the tough job, carrying mounds of brown mud to women who stroked it on by hand in the traditional manner, giving the pinkish, uneven, rounded walls the look of human skin. "Every inch was smoothed by a woman's hand," Georgia remarked about her house, enjoying the way its textured softness looked against the hard desert sky. "I wanted to make it my house [not Spanish or Indian or contemporary]. It is very hard to make the earth your own." She called it a carapace that fit her precisely. To villagers, it looked like a fortress that commanded Abiquiu's best view. "My home is simple, but I aim to make it simpler."

The places that captivate mature women are deliberately a world apart from traditional men's creation and company. "It may be that I am using the natural world as an escape from the world of men, but oh what a lovely escape it is," Martha Gellhorn wrote. And when she mourned in her increasing age "the lost world of her male friendships," she sublimated everything into a love affair with places.

A center is a part of, and apart from.

O'Keeffe seemed to levitate above the concerns of most mortals as she immersed herself in the grandeur of nature. The celestial purity of her work—her vision—was due to her detached and isolated life in the desert. She took no art students and lived with two fierce chows. And yet Ghost Ranch also became a platform upon which to be self-centered and "of service." O'Keeffe didn't hesitate to spar with people, especially the local priest, as she sought to do good in her community. She built a water system for the town, schools, and other public destinations. Her house looked like a fortress, but she was an important part of the community.

Madame de Maintenon was married at age forty-seven to Louis XIV, who was the same age. Her goal was "to make good use of my happiness." She founded a school of piety inside Louis's court, which was a mixture of vice, cynicism, and childlike credulity. While Louis's court was suffocating under peplums and laces and feasts, she avoided all ostentation. Her school for introducing poor girls to the court was a bit of radical genius. It did not change the court, but shook up its regulars. She took it upon herself to lecture the king on "the emptiness of greatness." She said she was the one person with whom the king "could be perfectly free."

A center teaches you what you are unable to exist without and so you find your essence.

"I think a house should just be a shelter," said O'Keeffe. The dry, desolate region in which she built her home contained nothing nourishing for the human body, only aesthetics for the soul—and she began to call it "the Black Place." A visitor marveled at the mood of "excited peace" in Georgia's home. It made superstitious townspeople wonder whether she was a witch, especially given the bones and a coiled snake in a recessed glass case, which once caused an Indian visitor to remark that everything in her home seemed alive, as if with supernatural spirits.

A center makes you feel safe.

Loss is no tragedy when a circle is extensive. It allows one to have an ongoing relationship with several hundred people and maintain an interlocking whole. Circles give a person the confidence to lose the unnecessary and gain the necessary.

In 1965 a fire destroyed O'Keeffe's uninsured paintings and other possessions. She said she had often wished for a fire to free her of possessions. She was reminded of what is important. For Georgia, that meant the act of painting. "[It] is what you do all the other things for...The painting is like a thread that runs through all the reasons for all the other things that makes one's life. When a tree dies you just have to plant two others."

The force of protectiveness extends to the fiscal nature of the matrix; modern matriarchies are distinct from most organizations: they are neither commercial nor charitable but a bit of both. Mead raised significant sums of money for her institutions while taking a small paycheck. Coco Chanel tutored hundreds of women in design while selling couture clothing. Gertrude Stein fed dozens of artists and supported their work by buying and displaying it. During World War II she drove her own car as an ambulance through the French countryside to transport the wounded to hospitals. Protectiveness reinforces the circular nature of matrixes: the French, honored by her presence, took exquisite care of Ms. Stein.

*A center encourages experiments, as a relief from the
lockstep world of laws and habits.*

Louise Nevelson was a compulsive arranger of furniture, objects, and boxes. She considered a house a
"live-in sculpture." She said, "If you're living with that
kind of harmony, something in the mind unfolds. Everything being a part of something larger and smaller
than itself against the theory of the infinite universe."

*A center blends love with friendship, the way a lit
candle shines in daylight.*

Eleanor Roosevelt created her circle within the circle
of her husband's presidential administration. Her court
was a conscience government, a parallel administration to FDR's. She did things that had never been done
before: she upset race traditions, championed a New
Deal for women, prevailed with legislation on housing
and the creation of model communities. Eleanor made
decisions and engineered policy. Her circle was staffed
with women; even the reporters she allowed to cover
her exclusively were women.

*A center is the autobiography of its key figure.
The link between the two is not leader-follower but
symbolic, iconic, and suggestive.*

Katharine Graham fretted at age forty-seven about
how to age gracefully: "We have to read a lot of books

and not drink," she told a friend, who, hearing this, became silent for a long time and then asked, "When do we have to start?"

Graham started when her husband committed suicide and she had to step quickly into his shoes as editor in chief of the family business, the Washington Post Company. She had held no professional role before. She had to recover from losing her husband and from the loss of confidence she had suffered throughout their twenty-three-year marriage, from his constant bullying and demeaning of her as unattractive and ordinary. Graham began to blossom as she entered an existing court and sought her place in it. She studied management, took advice from a lot of outsiders, partied with a new circle of peers that included the writer and bon vivant Truman Capote, and was not deterred by the endless criticism she heard from inside the *Post*. As befits one who seeks the center of a circle as opposed to the top of a pyramid, she did not govern, she enabled. She gave reporters unprecedented freedom. She became the middle ground, like a queen, between her staff and the power brokers of Washington. As Graham flourished in her position, the *Post* too, almost symbiotically, rose in visibility, prestige, and assumed a new stature, achieving its potential as a power nearly the equal of government to legislate moral code, the true fourth estate. The more Graham submitted to her role, the greater her power. She eventually unseated a corrupt president, Richard Nixon, by publishing the unnerving stories of the Watergate break-in he sanctioned. She ushered in a golden age of the credibility of the press. She led the *Post* to record years of profit and worldwide prestige.

There is one degree of separation for she who is at the center.

Penelope, queen of Ithaca, liked being in the center of the spider's web because there one isn't caught, one is in command, meaning in touch with all. A matriarch may also be slightly removed: Diane de Poitiers was the embodiment of the coolly maternal and hotly sexual. She had the word "Seule" engraved over her bed. The king was her lover but she always slept alone. Colette, too, desired "closeness without engulfment and a solitude that is not felt as abandonment."

Perhaps the most solo of modern matriarchs was Carolyn Heilbrun, founder of the women's studies programs—circles that are now staples of college life and the education of young women. Heilbrun saved time and gave herself room by announcing late in life that she would no longer give dinner parties. She ordered her clothes from catalogs and dressmakers. She did not waste her time squeezing fruit at supermarkets. It was a Maoist approach to her social life, ordaining that her meetings with friends should be almost wholly restricted to one-on-one affairs to limit idle chitchat. She left her teaching job at Columbia. She took a cottage all for herself on weekends, although she cherished her husband. She made herself the center of circles—academic, artistic, philanthropical. She believed that "an old woman may well for the first time be woman herself."

The icon at the center may withdraw from time to time, to no ill effect or diminishment of her power. Matriachies are full of reflected light. The novelist Willa Cather remarked that you cannot paint sunlight, you can only paint what it does with shadows on a wall. This is a perfect image of the widest effect of circles as organizational forms: if you examine a life, as Socrates said you must, do you really examine the life or the shadows it casts on other lives? Consider a glass prism, a little ball or cone found in any souvenir shop. It is never as beautiful as the rainbows it refracts. The perfect circle transforms people in it into Fours.

"Women are the more durable sex; they're made for surviving and holding things together." As there is never too much love and friendship, there are never too many circles.

The art of the comeback requires that
you reject any attempt to be young and
instead make the old new.

The culminating tactic requires combining the pre-
ceding tactics into one, the way light covers all
objects yet grants them greater individual presence.
A woman who totals up the hidden powers Leonardo
poured into his iconic woman stages the most precious
entrance of all: the comeback. Not just any old return,
but a presence that assures all observers that *they* went
missing, not she: your comeback is others' awakening
to your full power.

How does a leader seem more than a person who has
in maturity hung on, she who has merely lasted? Or to
use the cherished term of the moment, "survived"—a
much misunderstood condition. Why would one want
merely to survive when your best years are before you?

A few strategic women return from a long walkabout, a disappearing act where they have perhaps left a profession or a satisfying job, shelved a dream, or taken the wrong path. Coco Chanel was such a woman: she made a lethally wrong political move and aligned herself with the Nazis at the outbreak of World War II, and made decisions equally disastrous about the financing of her company. By such errors, she lost everything: her clients' goodwill, her friends' understanding, her company's carefully wrought image. At age seventy, however, she made a stunning return to the heights of the international fashion scene by reclaiming her essential gift—designing—and reintroducing her old original styles. There are dozens of similar stories of women long lost and forgotten finding themselves freshly admired in their fifties, sixties, seventies, or eighties. For women who want to return to that missed feast of the full promise of their lives, look at how they do so in age, when the world seems intent on counting them out once and for all. The tenth tactic completes this promise: that in maturity a woman is at last the sum total of all her talents, including those that have long been dormant.

If Joan of Arc had lived to fifty, would she have become a female pope and created a benign church? If Oprah were to assume a higher presence in life, run for the office of the president of the United States, for example, might she become a figure that is Reaganesque and Clintonesque both? We may imagine a very different world run by women who do not shy away from the feminine heart of leadership, who understand its losses and do not try to act like men.

* * *

Using any number or all ten tactics extends a leader's reach. The Stratagem affords three levels of power:

1. a mysterious presence
2. a doubled range of gender authority
3. four masks of increasingly mature command

To act upon this expanded sense of presence are specific tactics:

- comedic heroism
- the demonstration, occasionally, of unleashed anger

To express this new sense of self across Time, memory, and political and cultural boundaries, one uses words and webs as "microphones" that magnify one's voice:

- gravitas and sweeping statements
- circles of influence

Combined, these form the Stratagem. Female and feminine leaders throughout history have used these practices and applications. But the Stratagem may be its most timely now. As the world's population ages, so does the leadership of the Fortune 500 and their clients. The biggest companies in the world are run by men; yet these are men in their mature years, for whom matters of legacy, relationships, and the dawning comedy of age sets in. Mature leaders are no longer *merely* heroic. They are beyond that adolescent stance. They are increasingly human, or vulnerable, empathetic, and painfully aware that the future will not include them. So the scales of competition shift from beating the pants off one another to ensuring that their human sacrifice—decades at work—will have paid off in the long term, as a legacy. They are asking themselves: Have I left behind anything of substance? Do I still have an influence? What efforts are worth my time when time is so limited? Would my children consider my legacy a good one?

The number of aging leaders is at an historic high with the ripening of the baby boom, making this not an Iron Age, a Bronze Age, or a Brazen Age of supreme Internet wealth. This is the beginning of the Age of Age and *anti-heroic leadership* characterized by maturing talents. It is as if a line has been drawn in Time. Throughout the 1990s and early 2000s, the new economy considered every manager and leader heroic somehow merely for wringing profits out of a stone. Manager X wrestled convention, stood alone, and invented some new and temporarily dazzling technology. Puppydog Y proved himself a David who brought down a Goliath corporation. Up-and-coming leader Z persisted and prevailed—until the next David came along. They all conquered something, they triumphed somehow. *The Prince*'s values of winning were more important than mothering, teaching, steadying, or enlightening. Under the spell of Machiavelli's strategic classic, and the great-great-grandsons of his readers, young masters of the universe became characters that made the boys in *Lord of the Flies* seem like good guys focused on some prize, not heathens who would tear the wings off butterflies. The young male archetype did more than celebrate war over genius. It created a template of power—pseudo-heroism—that blinded many to their own flaws. One case in point: a world-famous investor and sudden philanthropist about to retire was once a middle-aged man as impulsive and spiteful as a child. Anyone who second-guessed him would be dismissed, and apologies or explanations never served this egomaniacal, iconic prince.

The hero narrative prevented outsiders from glimpsing the lethal immaturity of corporate leaders, at least until Tyco, Enron, MCI, and others exploded in scandal. But it also keeps leaders blindly faithful to a unipolar psychology of leadership: they had to be princely heroes; there was no other acceptable expression of power. A leader who despised female qualities as weak dismissed women as either "breeders" who give up their careers to start families or "greeters" who, whatever their professional acumen, serve the primary function of wooing or calming customers. "Even the most principled guys think of women as second rate," he said.

But this was before biology matured both women and men into more feminine creatures than ever before. In our new maturity, sticking to princely virtues is to use the tools of the last war to fight a new one—and thus going forth woefully unprepared. *The Prince* does not suit the age of Queens. Princes cannot address such questions as: What about the long haul? How do you find your destiny? What comes after the narrative of survival?

These questions can be answered by a success narrative that includes the anti-heroic elements. We may think of President Harry S. Truman as the case in point, the last president not to have a college education; a haberdasher by profession, he liked being characterized as an ordinary man. Throughout history, men in their mature years become more like Stratagem figures. They display the essential feminine qualities:

- a conscious turning away from the heroic to the ordinary, à la Truman;
- a healing anger, directed not toward competitors or only toward enemies but toward things as they are, as exemplified by the mature Winston Churchill;
- a willingness to engage with opportunities at an almost childlike level of submission and creativity, as we see in the case of the pianist Glenn Gould, whose last recording of *The Goldberg Variations* is almost a plaintive lullaby. Or the mature artist Titian throwing away his brushes and painting his last canvases with his thumbs;
- a display of emotions that opens them up to sentiment, not merely sweet reason, as we increasingly see in former presidents and now world-changing diplomats Jimmy Carter and Bill Clinton;
- a respect for feminine qualities in themselves and a growing impatience with the old male/female divide, which we note in each of these examples mentioned;
- a view of the world as increasingly comic and less and less tragic—the one element leaders need to cultivate much more.

It has been said that Bill Clinton was America's first female president: he was collaborative, often talked of love, and practiced a politics of sharing the nation's wealth. Yet recently, Clinton appears humbled after his heart surgery as he had never been humbled in his defiant younger years by the Monica Lewinsky fiasco and the ensuing impeachment trial. One may wonder how the full expression of this new sentimentality may deepen and extend his leadership. Could he find a language—a female gravitas—in which to express this emerging element of his character, and which might be even more persuasive than anything seen from him to date? The gender divide in leadership is not as significant, I believe, as the age divide.

I have known the feminine heart of leadership to beat in men and in women. In men it is something of a surprise, but beautiful. Parker Palmer, the educator, in lecturing Congress on the heartbreak of politics, is such a leader. Andy Grove in his mature years relented in such habits as teaching his executives the angry-wolf policy (Intel managers were taught to get under a colleague's nose and scream up into his or her nostrils their ideas and opinions). Grove softened and mellowed to the point where he could entertain uncertainty and ambiguity and new ideas in markets. Steve Jobs would walk incognito through the Apple parking lot to caress the surfaces of cars that were most beautiful, particularly the rounded forms, to deepen his quest to make technology that looked and felt human, perhaps even feminine: iPods have a "flick the bean" dial.

* * *

So how best to pull together all the tactics into a whole in which a One may advance into a Two, and a Two into a Three, et cetera, and we may become more mature as leaders?

A One becomes a Two by focusing on the tactic of cool eros. Adding an aspect of teacherliness to the basic human narcissism will detach a One from her ego. She becomes more powerful than she has become by boosting her attractiveness. The ancient painter Xerxes laughed himself to death while painting the portrait of an older woman. Even today, Susan Sontag noted, "Society allows no place in our imagination for a beautiful old woman who does look like an old woman. No one imagines such a woman exists." But she does exist. A One sees that uncentering the self gains a woman more power.

A Two advances to a Three by confronting the limits of her teaching. She indulges in the comic relief of feminine leadership and lightens her being. She indulges too in a submission to the random events of her life. She submits to being guided by the small odd force, like the buzzing fly in Inanna's experience. The small things change our lives more often than the big events. If there was any mysticism in Margaret Mead at all, it was in her tendency to "move with the tide of small events that seem to be deciding what to do next, with the general belief that the small events will give me the right cues. I follow the way the waves are rolling." She always looked for a new city, a new discipline, a new group to provide an abrupt and refreshing contrast with the one before.

A Three attains the level of a Four by expanding her vision. So she focuses on sweeping statements and sentiment and the building of circles. Pleasure is a subversive tactic for her.

A Four sustains her Fourness by knowing what a woman has to bear, and knowing that only at forty-five or fifty does she begin to acquire the courage to bear it, to take risks, make noise, be courageous, become unpopular. She knows that by doing so, she will be loved.

To tame Time by the means of the Stratagem is to buy oneself more time. The women who model the Stratagem turn out to be very patient. They have long periods of gestation—their youths and middle years—and then they flower. They *make haste slowly*.

* * *

There is a tale that on her deathbed Ann Richards, one-term governor of Texas, felt she had not achieved all she could have achieved. But unlike many in that proverbial situation who lament that they were not better husbands, fathers, or sons, Richards fretted that she had not been bold enough. Had she expressed her true strength, she would have given the powers that be in Texas a real run for their money. If she had stood up with all feminine and ferocious power to George Bush in his successful run to unseat her as governor for a second term, she might have kept her seat and thus kept him from the White House, which would have maintained her party's congressional dominance over social reforms. She did not remain true to her commitment to the I-word, meaning the fortune to *intimidate*.

The great women have a gift for knowing how far a woman can go—how intimidating she can be and still be loved. To be mature is to arrive at one's fullness and not be frightened of it.

What keeps women from recognizing our maturity at any age? The paucity of grown-up men.

What is a grown-up man? He who is not intimidated by grown-up, mature women. To put a finer point on it: he who runs a newspaper, perhaps like the *New York Times*, in which he refuses to run a caption for a photograph of singer Tony Bennett surrounded by two women in showgirl costumes in which he refers to them as "friends" of the singer. Aren't they performers too? How good would this aging crooner look without these women to contribute their dazzle?

But that's a simple case. Let's consider a tougher one: a woman at age fifty-two talked with a CEO about her ideas for reviving his company. She had been working for herself successfully for nearly ten years and now wanted to leave a bigger footprint in the sand, as one may do when one has the platform of a company. The CEO liked what she had to say. She had dressed for the meeting like a One, in Happy Hooker patterned panty-hose, a deliriously fluffy cashmere sweater, and a short skirt carried off with a humorous, slightly self-mocking touch, a little Julia Child, a little Anna Wintour. She showed up intending to look not sensible as a young woman might feel constrained to do; but rather as if she had earned the right to be entirely female.

This very adult man was grateful. He said, "I'd like you to join us, but I'm going to have to put you in front of someone at my company who won't be intimidated by you."

It wasn't the first time she had been stopped cold by the I-word. All she could think was, "You have a failing company, why wouldn't you want your people to be intimidated by me?"

The I-word makes it tough for mature women to use their full powers. And by this measure, you will know you are in possession of your full powers when you conjure that word. You have arrived. When you hear it, ask, "What do you mean by intimidating?" You will draw out a list of the most powerful qualities a woman may have.

But maturity is only partly about the I-word. The ancient philosopher Cicero asked himself what age was good for. In an essay *On Old Age*, he listed what he was happiest to be without. He said he was happy to have lost the strength of his muscles and the fury of his ambitions, because these took him away from the pleasures of the mind, which increased once he did not have to farm or build things. He was happiest to have gotten too knowing to be swept up by the fantasies of romantic love:

> That was a fine answer of Sophocles to a man who asked him, when in extreme old age, whether he was still a lover. "Heaven forbid!" he replied; "I was only too glad to escape from that, as though from a boorish and insane master."

Cicero found friendship (like Arendt's "amor mundi") more important over time than romantic love. But what makes him happiest in age? It is having one more day, and one more day, and one more...

And really, how should one use these days? Shakespeare's old King Lear said, "I will do such things, what they are yet I know not, but they shall be the terrors of the earth." He said this in impotent rage in his old age. But a practitioner of the Stratagem may say it in the brave beauty of age, submitting to its gifts.

There are women who return to the world stage after a long hiatus. One thinks of Alice Coltrane, widow of the jazz great John Coltrane. Alice swept into 'Trane's life the way Yoko swept into John Lennon's. She became his closest musical colleague and was despised for it. She did not return to the studio until age sixty-seven, twenty-four years after she released her last album. The final work was a going-against in the true form: she did not care about a market, she did not care about being faithful to her roots. She explored a sound that was a strange blend of Eastern sitar and piano-based gospel music. What might you do with the Stratagem? Stage your own comeback? Model a new form of leadership? Get out from your reclusive retirement and become interested again in making a difference?

When Sleeping Beauty woke up, she was really fifty years old, though she hardly realized it. You may realize how wonderful it is to wake up at fifty after the long sleep of youth. If you choose to do nothing, do it happily. The art of becoming legendary is the art of living another day. And so we make our truce with Time.

> *What stays with you latest and deepest? of curious*
> *   panics*
> *Of hard-fought engagements or sieges tremendous*
> *   what deepest remains?*
>
> —WALT WHITMAN

The Stratagem

Women are more themselves in age than at any
other time. They locate realms of permanence
in the world. They create love that constantly renews
itself. They engage in actions that are impervious
to forces of decay and disintegration. By such
means, Lioness and Lamb become one, and the
feminine heart of leadership prevails.

ACKNOWLEDGMENTS

Every book is really one long acknowledgment, and here are the names of those whose lines arose in a dinner conversation, an e-mail, and sometimes in shouts and whispers.

Thanks especially to Virginia Simpson, who says what she believes with a forensic exactitude that blends compassion and insight. Thanks multitudinously to Eric Walsh, physician, teacher, healer (though he dislikes the term), magus, musician, and schmaltzy Irish punster. A man who lives by his conviction that women are more powerful than men is a rare creature. I could write a book about all that Eric has taught me; perhaps that is the sum and substance of this book.

Thanks also to the Sisters of Mercy in Portland, Oregon, especially Crofton Diack, Ellen Fagg, Amy Archer, and all of the Serrato 17. Thanks to Win McCormack, who knows how to hone a girl's edge.

My agents Lynn Chiu and Glen Hartley are my stalwarts. I've been so lucky in a collaboration with the incomparable editor and publisher, Jamie Raab, Elle Exijente of Warner, and her team, Sharon Krassney and Ben Greenberg. And to Maureen Egen, whom I worshipped as a baby editor and still think of as the First Lady of Publishing.

Thanks to Anne Lim O'Brien of Heidrick & Struggles for her valuable time and to Dr. Patricia Allen, whose Menopause Ball in 2005 was an eye-opener—two hundred women in ballgowns without men to hog all the eye contact. Lori Bitter at S. Walter Thompson provided insight into age and markets. Dr. Ilse Lowenstam sends weekly letters that keep me eager for my own ninth decade. Betty Sue Flowers is a modern-day Eleanor of Aquitaine with a presence that is all poetry. Trace Goss has given me her Goss-pel to live by. John Campbell has been the lovingest hellhound a woman can have to watch her back. The pleasure of Martin Hynes's conversation and friendship made real to me what George Sand must have felt when she wrote to the much younger and better genius Gustave Flaubert.

And to Mona Rinzler Scheraga: I would be beyond thanking anybody if not for her. I grew up very poor, very lost, and quiet as a mouse. Mrs. Rinzler put a blank sheet of paper in front of her high-school kids and said, *Write*. I once thought that she taught us how to build a sentence. But more crucially, she taught us who she was: an unfailing optimist, a canny reader of souls, and a woman who knows how to flaunt her abundant curls and make the room she is in the most exciting place to be: she is a true Four. I was lucky enough to meet Mona in the tenth grade and to have found her again now that I am in the forty-seventh grade. Mona, you started my love affair with books that made life grand. It won't surprise you that I am still trying to fill a blank page that's good enough for you.

NOTES

p. vii   From Colette's biographer Radiguet, in Judith Thurman, *Secrets of the Flesh: A Life of Colette* (New York: Ballantine Books, 2000), 479.

Contents

p. xi   *The body is subject . . . ruled by levity*: Saul Bellow, *Collected Stories* (New York: Farrar, Straus and Giroux, 2002).

p. xi   *bring forth tigers*: quotation from Martha Gellhorn, in Caroline Moorehead, *Gellhorn: A Twentieth-Century Life* (New York: Owl Books, 2004).

Where May We Find Great Leaders Today?

pp. xiii–xiv Condoleezza Rice and Oprah: Maureen Dowd, "Who's Hormonal...?" *New York Times*, February 8, 2006.

Jackie's Immortal Godmothers

p. 1   On Madame de Maintenon: Eleanor Herman, *Sex with Kings* (New York: HarperCollins, 2005), 23.

p. 2   *resurgence*: Edward W. Said, *On Late Style: Music and Literature Against the Grain* (New York: Pantheon, 2006), 44.

p. 3   *salonistes*: Benedetta Craveri, *The Age of Conversation* (New York: New York Review of Books Collections, 2005).

p. 5   *for female writers . . . only after an awakening*: Carolyn G. Heilbrun, *Writing a Woman's Life* (New York: Ballantine Books, 1989), 117.

p. 7   *persons through whose hands . . . pass*: quotation from Madame D'Orleans, Princesse de Paphlagonia, in George Eliot, *Selected Essays, Poems and Other Writings* (New York: Penguin Classics, 1991), 23.

NOTES

pp. 10–11 Nevelson facts: Laurie Lisle, *Louise Nevelson: A Passionate Life* (New York: Ballantine Books, 2001), 208.

p. 11   *a thousand destructions*: ibid., 222.

p. 15   *Youth is a pathology . . . nonfailure*: Marilynne Robinson, *The Death of Adam: Essays on Modern Thought* (New York: Picador, 2005), 82–85.

p. 16   *thinker's flow*: James Wood, "Acts of Devotion," *New York Times Book Review*, November 28, 2004.

p. 16   Goldie and Greta: Claudia Roth Pierpont, *Passionate Minds: Women Rewriting the World* (New York: Knopf, 2001), 92–93.

p. 17   *discard the fantasy . . . for the reality*: ibid.

p. 17   *praised for what had been blamed for*: quotation from Margaret Mead, in Jane Howard, *Margaret Mead: A Wife* (New York: Fawcett, 1985).

p. 18   Hadid as everyone's Alfred Hitchcock: Herbert Muschamp, "Woman of Steel," *New York Times*, March 28, 2004.

p. 21   Men who helped George Eliot: Ruby Redinger, *George Eliot: The Emergent Self* (New York: Knopf, 1977), 472.

p. 21   *With submission comes self-mastery*: ibid., 478.

Tactic 1

p. 27   Quote on loss, immortality, and invulnerability loosely from Simon Schama, *Rembrandt's Eyes* (New York: Knopf, 1999), 61.

p. 28   *We wake every day . . . repeat the job*: Stephen Dobyns, "Rootless," in *Body Traffic* (New York: Penguin Poets, 1991).

p. 29   *The health and success . . . correspondence to its time*: Said, *On Late Style*.

p. 29   Quotation from George Sand in *Flaubert/Sand: The Correspondence*, translated from the French by Francis Steegmuller and Barbara Bray (New York: Knopf, 1993).

p. 35   *Beloved Shakespeare*: *Emily Dickinson Letters* (1884), 350.

p. 35   *Her losses make our gains ashamed*: ibid. (1885), 356.

pp. 36–39 Inanna story: Diane Wolkstein and Samuel Noah Kramer, *Inanna* (New York: HarperPerennial, 1983).

p. 41   Notion of life extending backwards: James Hillman, *The Force of Character and the Lasting Life* (New York: Ballantine Books, 2000), 27.

NOTES

p. 42   Maturity judging itself by the past: T. S. Eliot, "Tradition and the Individual Talent," *The Sacred Wood: Essays on Poetry and Criticism,* 6th ed. (London: Methuen, 1948).

p. 43   On an icon like a cell phone: Peter Schjeldahl, "Striking Gold," *The New Yorker,* May 17, 2004.

p. 44   Sand in *Flaubert/Sand,* 359.

Tactic 2

p. 51   *One's primary ground of meaning . . . to the soul:* Hillman, *Force of Character,* xvi.

p. 54   Story of cat onstage: Uta Hagen with Haskel Frankel, *Respect for Acting* (New York: Wiley, 1973).

p. 56   Wallace Stegner fictionalized his meeting with Dinesen in *The Spectator Bird* (New York: Penguin, 1990), 27.

p. 58   *Age . . . herself:* Heilbrun, *Writing a Woman's Life.*

p. 58   *Let your past . . . ripe:* Thurman, *Secrets of the Flesh.*

p. 59   *I love my present . . . :* Colette writing as Lea in *Cheri and the Last of Cheri* (New York: Ballantine Books, 1982).

p. 59   *We don't make mistakes:* Thurman, *Secrets of the Flesh,* 280.

p. 59   Stories of Catherine: Henri Troyat, *Catherine the Great* (New York: Berkley), 350–52.

pp. 59–60 *Content yourself with a passing temptation . . . :* Colette quoted in Thurman, *Secrets of the Flesh,* 305.

Tactic 3

p. 62   Older women privy to men's cult secrets: Hillman, *Force of Character,* 13.

p. 63   *The privilege a woman has:* Thurman, *Secrets of the Flesh,* 354.

p. 64   Batali anecdote: Bill Buford, *Heat: An Amateur's Adventures as Kitchen Slave, Line Cook, Pasta-Maker, and Apprentice to a Dante-Quoting Butcher in Tuscany* (New York: Knopf, 2006), 13.

p. 66   *One does not so much seduce a boy . . . :* Thurman, *Secrets of the Flesh,* 303.

p. 67   Narrative of invitation: George Lakoff quoted in Matt Bai, "The Framing Wars," *New York Times Sunday Magazine,* July 17, 2005.

NOTES

p. 67   *mastery of the master*: Susan Hardy Aiken, *Isak Dinesen and the Engineering of Narrative* (Chicago: University of Chicago Press, 1990), 11.

p. 68   Non-elephants and Ségolène Royal: James Traub, "La Femme," *New York Times Sunday Magazine*, May 14, 2006.

p. 69   *Some cultures burn such women . . . Others elect them queens*: Mary Tannen, "Appearances: For Mature Audiences," *New York Times Sunday Magazine*, January 22, 2006.

p. 71   *unproductive productiveness*: Said, *On Late Style*, 7.

Tactic 4

p. 74   *When you feel your own "self" . . .* : Sand in *Flaubert/Sand*, 56–57.

p. 75   Kinds of beauty inspired: Victor Turner, *The Anthropology of Performance* (Baltimore: PAJ Publications, 1986).

p. 76   Anecdote about Eleanor Roosevelt: Joseph Lash, *Eleanor: The Years Alone* (New York: Simon & Schuster, 1986), 50.

p. 77   Colette on flowering: Thurman, *Secrets of the Flesh*, 497.

p. 79   On Nevelson: Lisle, *Louise Nevelson*, 265 and 269.

p. 80   Interpretation of *Antony and Cleopatra*: Harold Bloom, *Shakespeare: The Invention of the Human* (New York: Riverhead Press, 1998).

p. 81   Nin biography: Pierpont, *Passionate Minds*, 69–72.

p. 87   Anecdote on de Wolfe: Thurman, *Secrets of the Flesh*, 479.

p. 88   *simultaneous dependence-independence*: Lewis Hyde, *The Trickster Makes This World: Mischief, Myth, and Art* (New York: Farrar, Straus and Giroux, 1998), 241.

p. 88   *caught in the gap between . . . and worldliness*: Edna O'Brien on Onassis, quoted in Sarah Bradford, *America's Queen: A Life of Jacqueline Kennedy Onassis* (New York: Viking, 2000), 431.

p. 90   O'Keeffe's face: Laurie Lisle, *Portrait of an Artist: A Biography of Georgia O'Keeffe* (New York: Pocket Books, 1986), 378.

p. 90   O'Keeffe's posture: ibid., 380.

p. 91   O'Keeffe's getting what she wanted: ibid., 325.

p. 91   *She has a shotgun . . .* : ibid., 321.

p. 91   O'Keeffe's self-centered attitude: ibid., 320.

NOTES

p. 95   Colette's appearance to her lover: Thurman, *Secrets of the Flesh,* 291–92.

p. 96   Colette's muscled body: ibid., 295.

p. 96   Description of Stein fictionalized in the voice of her cook: Monique Truong, *The Book of Salt: A Novel* (New York: Houghton Mifflin, 2003), 28.

pp. 99–100 Jordan and Ann Richards: Mary Beth Rogers, *Barbara Jordan: American Hero* (New York: Bantam, 2000), 339.

p. 100   Jordan and Bible: ibid., 341.

p. 102   Gellhorn on Roosevelt: Moorehead, *Gellhorn,* 81.

p. 103   *Time and Space*: Strindberg quoted in Susan Sontag, *New York Times Book Review*, February 20, 2005.

Tactic 5

p. 110   *a sudden wave of cold air*: Kenneth Clark and Martin Kemp, *Leonardo da Vinci,* rev. ed. (New York: Penguin, 1989), 120.

p. 110   *a person and a woman both*: Thurman, *Secrets of the Flesh*, xvii.

p. 110   *an erotic galaxy* . . . : loosely quoted from Thurman, *Secrets of the Flesh*, 481.

p. 111   *It is the mother's . . . that man exists for her*: loosely quoted from T. H. White, *The Once and Future King* (New York: Ace, 1987), 611–12.

p. 111   The lap of Margaret Mead and her fame: Howard, *Margaret Mead,* xiv.

p. 112   *From ancient times to modern:* quoting Geza Roheim in Wendy Doniger, *The Woman Who Pretended to Be Who She Was: Myths of Self-Imitation* (Oxford: Oxford University Press, 2006), 143.

p. 112   *If mothers were to cast off their skins*: ibid.

p. 113   Biography of O'Keeffe: Lisle, *Portrait of an Artist,* 405.

p. 113   Juan Hamilton facts: ibid., 409–10.

p. 114   Sand/Flaubert letters: *Flaubert/Sand*, 48.

p. 116   Facts about Ellen Johnson-Sirleaf: Jon Lee Anderson, "Letter from Liberia," *The New Yorker*, March 27, 2006, 65.

p. 117   *Man has finally been shorn* . . . : Colette biographer Sarde on his subject at age fifty, quoted in Heilbrun, *Writing a Woman's Life,* 84.

NOTES

p. 117 Young men and Colette: Thurman, *Secrets of the Flesh*, 297 and 382.

p. 117 *young people "[back] away . . . ruled by love"*: Thurman explicating Colette's novel *The Last of Cheri*, ibid., 352.

p. 118 *We who forbade*: Karmen MacKendrick, *Counterpleasures* (Albany: State University of New York Press, 1999).

p. 118 *To gain pleasures*: ibid.

p. 119 Pleasure and the structure of power: ibid., 17.

p. 120 Nevelson's admirers: Lisle, *Louise Nevelson*, 285.

pp. 120–21 Saints, pleasure, and ascetic life: MacKendrick, *Counterpleasures*, 14–15.

p. 121 On Bertrand: Thurman, *Secrets of the Flesh*, 296.

pp. 121–22 Lea and Cheri: ibid., 290.

p. 122ff. On Catherine: Troyat, *Catherine the Great*, 165–67.

p. 124 Catherine's pursuit of the ideal companion: ibid., 282.

p. 124 Little Mother Catherine: ibid., 400.

Tactic 6

p. 126 *Like Christ . . . beautiful things to her*: Oscar Wilde, *De Profundis and Other Writings* (London: Penguin Classics, 1976).

p. 126 *A smile communicates pleasure . . . power*: Mikhail Bakhtin, *Rabelais and His World* (Bloomington: Indiana University Press, 1984), 93.

p. 128 *the mysterious personal force that commands*: Northrop Frye, *A Natural Perspective* (New York: Columbia University Press, 1995), 71.

p. 128 Living with suffering: ibid., 143.

p. 130 born women: Heilbrun, *Writing a Woman's Life*, 131.

p. 130 Blixen as a writer: Hannah Arendt, *Men in Dark Times* (New York: Harvest Books, 1970), 96.

pp. 130–31 *brooches*: Madeleine Albright, *Madame Secretary: A Memoir* (New York: Miramax Books, 2003).

p. 132 Truth and comedy: Diana Vreeland, *DV* (Cambridge, MA: Da Capo Press, 2003), 165.

p. 132 *To be cool and calm . . .* : interview with Haruki Murakami, "The Art of Fiction," *Paris Review*, no. 170, Summer 2004.

p. 133   *a major woman . . . Lucille Ball*: Betty Fussell, *My Kitchen Wars* (Berkeley: North Point Press, 2000).

p. 134   Quotation from Diana Vreeland, *DV*, 143.

p. 135   Mead anecdote: Howard, *Margaret Mead*, 375.

p. 136   Power and laughter: Bakhtin, *Rabelais and His World*, 45.

p. 136   Coping with a future: Suzanne Langer, "The Comic Rhythm," in *Comedy: Meaning and Form*, 2nd ed., Robert W. Corrigan, ed. (New York: Harper & Row, 1981), 70.

p. 136   Quotation from George Sand in *Flaubert/Sand*, 155.

p. 138   *dreams are realer than real*: Frye, *A Natural Perspective*, 130.

p. 138   *to reveal something wisdom doesn't see*: ibid., 118.

p. 139   Eleanor Roosevelt quoted in Lash, *Eleanor*, 29.

pp. 139–40 On the past: Galen Strawson on narrative, "A Fallacy of Our Age," *Times Literary Supplement*, October 15, 2004.

p. 141   Menachem–Golda exchange in William Gibson, *Golda's Balcony: A Play* (New York: Applause Books, 2003), 39.

pp. 141–42 Comment about the Arabs: ibid., 60.

p. 143   *intricate spiritual choreography*: Bloom, *Shakespeare*, 207.

p. 144   *no happiness*: ibid., 211–12.

p. 144   *erotic realist*: ibid.

p. 144   *To undo power . . . restores what is missing*: George Lakoff quoted in Bai, "The Framing Wars."

Tactic 7

p. 146   *Hate and wait*: Princess Michael of Kent, *The Serpent and the Moon: Two Rivals for the Love of a Renaissance King* (New York: Simon & Schuster, 2004).

p. 147   *Widowhood alone would be hers*: ibid.

p. 147   *learn to fashion history according to her own needs*: Leonie Frieda, *Catherine de Medici: Renaissance Queen of France* (New York: Fourth Estate, 2005), 9.

pp. 147–48 Sontag quoted in Craig Seligman, *Sontag and Kael: Opposites Attract Me* (New York: Counterpoint Press, 2005), 111.

p. 148   *in the prize ring of life . . .* : Thurman, *Secrets of the Flesh*, 365.

p. 149   Colette on being a monster and a saint: ibid., xi.

p. 150   *Character . . . hardened*: ibid., 365.

NOTES

pp. 150–51 Edith Wharton facts: R. W. B. Lewis, *Edith Wharton: A Biography* (New York: HarperCollins, 1975), 217ff.

p. 153   Quotation and reading of Penelope's story: Margaret Atwood, *The Penelopiad: The Myth of Penelope and Odysseus* (New York: Canongate Books, 2005), 119.

pp. 160–61 Wallace T. MacCaffrey, *Elizabeth I: War and Politics 1588–1603* (Princeton, NJ: Princeton University Press, 1992).

p. 163   *Women have lived too much with closure*: Vanessa Grigoriadis, "A Death of One's Own," *New York Magazine*, December 8, 2003.

p. 163   *Doubt is very laming to the young*: Barbara Hannah, *The Inner Journey: Lectures and Essays on Jungian Psychology* (Toronto: Inner City Books, 1999), 122.

p. 163   *When you are not enclosed by closure*: Heilbrun, *Writing a Woman's Life*, 130.

p. 164   *do not make a new life; they rearrange what is already at hand*: Hyde, *The Trickster Makes This World*, 341.

p. 164   *A blow . . . a caress*: Sand in *Flaubert/Sand*, 245.

Tactic 8

p. 166   *artful artlessness*: Elizabeth Wanning Harries, *Twice Upon a Time: Women Writers and the History of the Fairy Tale* (Princeton, NJ: Princeton University Press, 2001), 63.

p. 166   *eloquence in silence*: Lance Morrow, "The Gravitas Factor," *Time*, March 14, 1988.

p. 167   Fallaci quotes from Margaret Talbot, "The Agitator," *The New Yorker*, June 5, 2006.

p. 169   Barbara Jordan quoted in Rogers, *Barbara Jordan*, 323.

pp. 169–70 Hannah Arendt's last words: Elisabeth Young-Bruehl, *Hannah Arendt: For Love of the World* (New Haven, CT: Yale University Press, 1983).

p. 171   Notes on *Uncle Tom's Cabin* drawn from discussion of the novel in Leslie Fiedler, *The Inadvertent Epic* (New York: Touchstone, 1980), 22–34.

p. 174   *If we are whole . . . we are old*: Barbara Jordan quoted in Rogers, *Barbara Jordan*, 322.

pp. 174–75 Observation of Jordan by Sandy Grady, ibid., 322–23.

NOTES

p. 179   William Shakespeare, *Antony and Cleopatra*, act IV, scene xv, lines 73–91.

p. 180   *the biofissure*: Bloom, *Shakespeare*.

p. 180   *unselfs the self*: Robinson, *The Death of Adam*, 82.

p. 181   *Women above all . . . How did we lose that?*: from personal correspondence, Virginia Simpson.

Tactic 9

p. 183   George Eliot, *Selected Essays*, 13.

p. 185   Circles in architecture: Muschamp, "Woman of Steel."

p. 186   *Matriarchies . . . the heart*: lecture on Emily Dickinson by Allen Grossman, "Poetry: A Basic Course," The Teaching Company audio recording, 1990.

p. 186ff.   Amy Ruth Kelly, *Eleanor of Aquitaine and the Four Kings* (Cambridge, MA: Harvard University Press, 1991), 158–63.

p. 187   *crystallizations of great ideas*: George Eliot, *Selected Essays*.

p. 189   The legend of Eleanor and Henry engaging in a mental chess game in their late years is captured in the film *The Lion in Winter*, directed by Anthony Harvey, 1968.

p. 190   *No king in Europe . . .* : Kelly, *Eleanor of Aquitaine*, 254.

pp. 190–91   Interpretation of Emily Dickinson: Richard Sewell, *The Life of Emily Dickinson* (New York: Farrar, Straus and Giroux, 1980), 617–18.

pp. 191–92   Horizons and confusion: Howard, *Margaret Mead*, 359.

pp. 192–93   Gertrude Stein comment: James Mellow, *Charmed Circle: Gertrude Stein and Company* (New York: Henry Holt and Co., 2003).

pp. 193–94   Mead quotes from Howard, *Margaret Mead*, 355–56.

pp. 195–200   Mead facts and quotes: ibid., 324 ff.

p. 197   *the sharp compassion of the healer's art*: T. S. Eliot, "East Coker," *Four Quartets* in *The Complete Poems and Plays, 1909–1950* (New York: Harcourt Brace & Co., 1980), 127.

p. 200   *happiness depends on people's experience of the ends of things*: Daniel Gilbert, *Stumbling on Happiness* (New York: Knopf, 2006).

p. 203   Nevelson quoted in Lisle, *Louise Nevelson*, 271.

[241]

NOTES

pp. 204–5 O'Keeffe's home of pink walls: Lisle, *Portrait of an Artist,* 327–29.

p. 205   Gellhorn's love of escape: Moorehead, *Gellhorn,* 326, 369, and 380.

pp. 205–6 Maintenon biography: Maud Cruttwell, *Madame De Maintenon* (London: Unwin Brothers, 1930).

p. 207   *the confidence to lose the unnecessary . . .* : Sand in *Flaubert/Sand,* 369.

p. 207   O'Keeffe's fire: Lisle, *Portrait of an Artist,* 397–98.

p. 207   *When a tree dies:* Sand in *Flaubert/Sand,* 226.

p. 208   Louise Nevelson: Lisle, *Louise Nevelson,* 270.

p. 208   Eleanor's circle: Blanche Wiesen Cook, *Eleanor Roosevelt: Volume Two, The Defining Years, 1933–1938* (New York: Viking, 1999), 3.

pp. 208–10 Katharine Graham, *A Personal History* (New York: Vintage, 1998), 391.

pp. 210–11 Facts on Carolyn Heilbrun's last years: Grigoriadis, "A Death of One's Own."

p. 211   Comment on sunlight: Stegner, *The Spectator Bird,* 162.

p. 211   Women as the more durable sex: ibid., 11.

Tactic 10

p. 221   *the courage . . . to take risks . . . be loved:* Heilbrun, *Writing a Woman's Life.*